Essential
GERMAN
VERB
SKILLS

Essential
GERMAN
VERB
SKILLS

ED SWICK

McGraw·Hill

New York   Chicago   San Francisco   Lisbon   London   Madrid   Mexico City
Milan   New Delhi   San Juan   Seoul   Singapore   Sydney   Toronto

The *McGraw-Hill* Companies

Library of Congress Cataloging-in-Publication Data

Swick, Edward.
    Essential German verb skills / by Ed Swick.
       p.   cm.
    Includes index.
    ISBN 0-07-145388-1
     1. German language—Verb.   2. German language—Textbooks for foreign
speakers—English.   I. Title.

    PF3271.S93   2005
    438.2'421—dc22   2005047723

1 2 3 4 5 6 7 8 9 0   FGR/FGR   0 9 8 7 6 5

ISBN 0-07-145388-1

Interior design by Nick Panos

McGraw-Hill books are available at special quantity discounts to use as premiums and sales promotions, or for use in corporate training programs. For more information, please write to the Director of Special Sales, Professional Publishing, McGraw-Hill, Two Penn Plaza, New York, NY 10121-2298. Or contact your local bookstore.

This book is printed on acid-free paper.

Contents

Acknowledgments

With much gratitude to Sabine McNulty for all her help and suggestions.

Introduction

You've been studying German for some time now and have paid your dues learning how to conjugate verbs. You know how to conjugate in all the tenses and are even comfortable conjugating the most common irregular verbs. You've now decided to take the next step in developing a mastery of German verb usage.

No doubt you've noticed that there is much more than just conjugation in understanding how verbs function in complete sentences. This point is where *Essential German Verb Skills* begins. *Essential German Verb Skills* will show you how to integrate verbs into meaningful sentences.

This book does not deal with basic tense formation since it presupposes that you have already covered this area sufficiently. This approach will allow you not to have to spend time repeating what you've already learned. Another aspect of the book that will enhance your studying is how it covers German verb usage by comparing it to English verb usage. All through the book, you will find constant references to how English functions in the particular topic presented, accompanied by clear explanations on how native German speakers express the same idea.

Essential German Verb Skills offers a wide variety of topics regarding correct verb usage in particular areas that often cause a lot of difficulty for English-speaking students. The book's clear explanations are supplemented by thorough examples. Each chapter also includes exercises that will enable you to practice and reinforce what you have just learned. You may then check your work in the Answer Key at the end of the book. Here you will also find a handy appendix of Quick-Glance Tables that will provide you with fast and practical clarifications of a number of important verb topics.

By the time you finish this book, you will find yourself well on your way to speaking and writing in German better than ever. *Viel Glück!*

Essential
GERMAN
VERB
SKILLS

Haben, sein, and werden

Having studied German, you are probably very familiar with the conjugations of **haben**, **sein**, and **werden**. These three verbs function in very important ways individually as conjugated verbs and in concert with one another and still in other ways with numerous other verbs. They are the building blocks of German verb tenses, voice, and mood.

Haben

The verb **haben** means *to have* and is used in the same way that the English verb is used. It indicates that someone possesses or controls someone or something.

*Meine Schwester **hat** jetzt fünf Kinder.*	My sister has five children now.
*Die Touristen werden morgen ein paar Stunden Freizeit **haben**.*	The tourists will have a few hours of free time tomorrow.

But the use of **haben** goes beyond its basic meaning of *to have*. **Haben** is also used in certain high-frequency expressions that do not change except for the subject, tense, or sometimes the object of the verb.

*Du **hast** Recht.*	You're right.
*Ich **habe** es satt!*	I'm sick of it!
*Karl **hat** die neue Studentin aus Italien gern.*	Karl likes the new student from Italy.

The expression **gern haben** (*to like*) also has its comparative and superlative forms: **lieber haben** (*to prefer, to like better*) and **am liebsten haben** (*to find most preferable, to like the most*).

Haben is also commonly used to express hunger and thirst where in English the verb *to be* is substituted for *to have*.

*Ich möchte etwas essen. Ich **habe** Hunger.*	I'd like something to eat. I'm hungry.
*Die Kinder **haben** Durst.*	The children are thirsty.

When not conjugated as an individual verb, *haben* is used together with past participles to form the present perfect, the past perfect, and the future perfect tenses. The present perfect tense requires a conjugation of *haben* in the present tense. The past perfect tense requires a conjugation of *haben* in the past tense. And the future perfect tense requires a conjugation of *werden* followed by a past participle and *haben* as an infinitive. Note in the following examples that *haben* acts as the auxiliary in the perfect tenses for verbs that take an accusative object or a dative object. Such verbs are called **transitive verbs**.

*Ich **habe** ihm dafür gedankt.*	I thanked him for it.
***Hatten** Sie das erwartet?*	Had you expected that?
*Bis Montag wird sie es geschrieben **haben**.*	By Monday she'll have written it.

It is also the auxiliary for the modal auxiliaries (*dürfen*, *können*, *mögen*, *müssen*, *sollen*, and *wollen*) and the verbs *helfen*, *hören*, *lassen*, *sehen*, *gehen*, and *lernen* when a double infinitive structure is required in the present perfect, past perfect, and future perfect tenses.

*Die Schüler **haben** die Übersetzung nicht schreiben können.*	The pupils haven't been able to write the translation.
*Mein Vetter **hat** den alten Mercedes reparieren lassen.*	My cousin had the old Mercedes repaired.

Haben is even used in very specialized phrases that evade the basic meaning of the verb. In accounting, for example, *Soll und Haben* is special jargon, which in English is translated as *debit and credit*.

Sein

The basic meaning of **sein** is *to be* when it is conjugated as an individual verb. This meaning is exemplified by a phrase from Shakespeare that is as well known in German as it is in English:

> *Sein oder nicht sein; das ist hier die*   To be or not to be; that is the
> *Frage.*   question.

In its imperative form, **sein** is used in numerous everyday expressions. The form **sei** is used as an imperative for **du**; **seid** is used for **ihr**; and **Seien Sie** is used for **Sie**.

Sei *zufrieden!*	Be content.
Sei *tapfer!*	Be brave.
Sei *artig!*	Be well behaved.

And, although German and English use the same verb to express the following idea, they do it in their own individual ways. In English the pronoun *it* is used with a conjugation of the verb *to be*. That phrase is followed by a personal pronoun to form this expression. But German conjugates **sein** with the pronoun subject and completes the phrase with **es**.

Ich **bin's**.	It's me.
Sind *Sie es?*	Is that you?

In certain other phrases, English uses the verb *to have* where German prefers **sein**.

der Ansicht **sein**	to have a point of view
des Glaubens **sein**	to have a belief
der Meinung **sein**	to have the opinion (to be of the opinion)

Notice that the German expressions above all require the nouns to be in the genitive case.

When a dative case object is used with **sein**, the English translation must often be *to feel*.

Was **ist** *Ihnen?*	What's the matter with you?

*Mir **ist** warm.*	I feel warm.
*Ihm **ist** schlecht.*	He doesn't feel well.

In the present perfect, past perfect, and future perfect tenses ***sein*** acts as the auxiliary of verbs of motion and of certain special verbs that describe a state, a condition, or a radical change. In these instances, the verb must be translated in English as *to have*.

*Die großen Hunde **sind** der armen Frau entlaufen.*	The large dogs have run away from the poor woman.
*Die alte Gräfin **war** vor einigen Tagen gestorben.*	The old countess had died some days ago.
*Er wird bis Mittag angekommen **sein**.*	He'll have arrived by noon.

And **sein** is the auxiliary for itself in those same tenses.

*Ich **bin** noch nicht da **gewesen**.*	I still haven't been there.

In the present perfect, past perfect, and future perfect tenses of the passive voice ***sein*** is always the auxiliary. Remember that the participle of a passive voice sentence is always ***worden*** and not ***geworden***.

*Die Geschenke **sind** von einem Freund von mir gebracht worden.*	The gifts have been brought by a friend of mine.
*Dem Rechtsanwalt **ist** für seine Hilfe von der Angeklagten gedankt worden.*	The lawyer has been thanked for his help by the defendant.

Whether the verb in a passive sentence requires an accusative object or a dative object, the verb ***sein*** is always the auxiliary of the participle. In the above examples, ***die Geschenke*** in the active sentence was the accusative object of the verb ***bringen***, and ***dem Rechtsanwalt*** in the active sentence was the dative object of the verb ***danken***. In the passive voice, ***sein*** is the auxiliary for both:

sind gebracht worden	*ist gedankt worden*

Werden

Conjugated as an individual verb, **werden** often means *to become*. The subject of this verb can be animate or inanimate.

Der junge Mann will Arzt **werden**.	The young man wants to become a doctor.
Die letzten zwei Tage **wurden** *regnerisch*.	The last two days became rainy.

Werden can also imply the meaning *to grow*.

Der Himmel ist dunkel **geworden**.	The sky has grown dark.

And it is even used as one translation for the English verb *to get*.

Es **wird** *kalt*.	It's getting cold.

Like **haben** and **sein**, **werden** is used in certain common expressions that are immediately understood by natives.

Die Tage **werden** *länger*.	The days are growing longer.
Der Kranke wird wieder **werden**.	The patient will make a complete recovery.
Es **wird** *Licht! Und es* **ward** *Licht!* (**ward** is poetical)	Let there be light! And there was light!
Gudrun **wird** *Mutter*.	Gudrun's going to have a baby.

An important function of **werden** is in the formation of the future tense. In a future tense construction, **werden** is conjugated, and an infinitive ends the sentence.

Werden *Sie Ihren Bruder in Mannheim besuchen?*	Will you visit your brother in Mannheim?

Werden is also an essential component of the passive voice. It is conjugated and accompanied by a transitive verb formed as a past participle.

Die Kinder **werden** *von einem neuen Lehrer unterrichtet*.	The children are being instructed by a new teacher.
Karl **wurde** *von Maria geküsst*.	Karl was kissed by Maria.

In the present perfect, past perfect, and future perfect tenses the participle of **werden** becomes **worden**. The participle **geworden** is used when the verb means *to become, get,* or *grow.*

Ihm ist für den Empfang gedankt **worden.**	He has been thanked for the reception.
Oma ist krank **geworden.**	Granny has become ill.

And if a passive voice sentence has as its main verb a modal auxiliary, the past participle and **werden** become a **passive infinitive**.

Die verlorenen Bücher müssen **gefunden werden.**	The lost books have to be found.

The verb **werden** has yet another unique task in the German language. It is used in the past subjunctive (subjunctive II) as the auxiliary of an infinitive much the way the English verb *would* is used.

Wenn die Alpen näher wären, **würden** *wir dorthin fahren.*	If the Alps were nearer, we would drive there.
Der Chef **würde** *ihn entlassen, wenn er schlecht arbeitete.*	The boss would fire him if he worked badly.

You will discover that **haben**, **sein**, and **werden** play a significant role in all aspects of German verbs. A good understanding of them is the key to success with topics taken up in this book.

Exercise 1
Fill in the blank with the appropriate form of **haben**, **sein**, or **werden**.

1. Der Amerikaner _____ seinen deutschen Freund besucht.

2. Gestern _____ ich keine Zeit dazu.

3. Wir wissen, dass du es nicht _____ lernen können.

4. Ich ＿＿＿＿＿＿＿ nicht der Ansicht.

5. Das Bild ist von dem Maler gemalt ＿＿＿＿＿＿＿.

6. Es ＿＿＿＿＿＿＿ sehr heiß.

7. Die Wunden ＿＿＿＿＿＿＿ von einem jungen Arzt geheilt.

8. Wen ＿＿＿＿＿＿＿ Sie gefragt?

9. ＿＿＿＿＿＿＿ ihr den ausländischen Studenten begegnet?

10. Wenn das Buch nicht interessant wäre, ＿＿＿＿＿＿＿ er es
    nicht lesen.

Word Order

In German, word order tends to follow strict patterns, and exceptions to the rules are quite rare, unlike how German gender is derived or the kinds of irregularities that exist in conjugations. Therefore, once you have learned the patterns of German word order, you can rely on them.

Although it may appear that many elements shift position in a German sentence, it is the verb that is affected most by word order. Verbs have a specific location in a sentence, which is determined by the kind of sentence used (statement or question) and by the tense and complexity of the verb.

The Present and Past Tenses

When there is a present or past tense verb in a statement, there is a simple rule to follow for word order: **the verb is always the second element in the statement.** The first element in a statement could be the subject of the sentence. It could be the direct object, or an adverb, or a prepositional phrase, or an entire clause with its own subject and verb. No matter what begins the sentence, the verb in a statement is always in the second position. Look at these examples of sentences that begin with a variety of elements. Notice that nouns are being used both as the subject and as the direct object of the sentences:

SUBJECT
***Der Mann** kaufte einen Mantel.*   The man bought a coat.

DIRECT OBJECT
***Einen Mantel** kaufte der Mann
im Kaufhaus.*   The man bought a coat in the department store.

ADVERB

Gestern kaufte der Mann einen Mantel.

Yesterday the man bought a coat.

PREPOSITIONAL PHRASE

In der Stadt kaufte der Mann einen Mantel.

The man bought a coat in the city.

ENTIRE CLAUSE

Als er in Berlin war, kaufte der Mann einen Mantel.

When he was in Berlin, the man bought a coat.

Whether the subject of a declarative sentence is a noun or pronoun and the direct object is a noun or pronoun, the same rule of word order applies: the conjugated verb is the second element in a sentence that is in the present or past tense.

SUBJECT

Wir besuchten Onkel Karl im Krankenhaus.

We visited Uncle Karl in the hospital.

DIRECT OBJECT

Das verstehe ich nicht.

I don't understand that.

ADVERB

Plötzlich verstehe ich das nicht.

Suddenly I don't understand that.

PREPOSITIONAL PHRASE

Im Krankenhaus besuchten wir Onkel Karl.

We visited Uncle Karl in the hospital.

ENTIRE CLAUSE

Obwohl er es erklärt, verstehe ich das nicht.

Although he's explaining it, I don't understand that.

But if a present or past tense verb is in a **question**, the verb will be either the first or the second word in the sentence. If the question is formed without an interrogative word, the verb will begin the question.

Notice that the verbs in the following examples are **haben**, **sein**, **werden**, a modal auxiliary, and a verb with an irregular present tense conjugation:

Hast *du genug Geld?*	Do you have enough money?
Ist *heute Mittwoch?*	Is today Wednesday?
Wird *sie krank?*	Is she getting sick?
Kann *sie Deutsch?*	Does she know German?
Liest *du einen Roman?*	Are you reading a novel?

If the question begins with an interrogative (**wer**, **wen**, **was**, **wo**, **warum**, etc.), then the verb is the second element in the question. The following questions all begin with an interrogative word:

Wo *wohnen deine Eltern jetzt?*	Where do your parents live now?
Warum *ist Ludwig immer so müde?*	Why is Ludwig always so tired?
Was *möchten Sie?*	What would you like?
Wer *wohnt in dem kleinen Haus?*	Who lives in the little house?
Wann *kommt der Zug?*	When is the train coming?

Notice that the subjects and objects in these example sentences can be either nouns or pronouns.

If the interrogative word is used as an adjective, it is most often followed directly by a noun (**welche Bluse**, **welches Haus**). But the combination of these two words is considered a single element (adjective + noun). The second element is still the verb.

Welche Bluse *willst du?*	Which blouse do you want?
Welches Haus *kauften sie?*	Which house did they buy?

The same is true of **wessen**.

Wessen Wagen *steht dort drüben?*	Whose car is over there?
Wessen Professor *geht in die Bibliothek?*	Whose professor is going to the library?

The Present Perfect

The present perfect tense is composed of a conjugation of **haben** or **sein** plus a past participle (**er hat gelacht, sie ist gekommen**). As the person and number of the subject of the sentence change, the verb **haben** is conjugated appropriately for transitive verbs, but the past participle remains constant, and the position of the past participle is always at the end of the sentence.

Ich habe meinen Fahrschein **verloren**.	I have lost my driver's license.
Hast du seinen alten VW **gekauft**?	Have you bought his old VW?
Sie haben Schach **gespielt**.	They have played chess.

As the person and number of the subject of a sentence that has a verb of motion change, the verb **sein** is conjugated, but the past participle remains constant and is located at the end of the sentence.

Du bist wieder krank **gewesen**.	You have been sick again.
Wir sind neulich **angekommen**.	We have recently arrived.
Seid ihr mit dem Bus **gefahren**?	Have you traveled by bus?

As you see in the examples above, the position of the past participle is not affected by the formation of the participle, whether regular or irregular, whether with a prefix or without a prefix. It remains at the end of the sentence.

When two independent clauses are combined with a coordinate conjunction, you have a **compound sentence**. In compound sentences the past participle is at the end of each clause.

Werner hat Bücher **gekauft**, *aber sein Bruder hat sein Geld* **gespart**.	Werner has bought books, but his brother has saved his money.

When some element other than the subject begins a sentence that is in the present perfect tense, the same rule applies that applies for a present or past tense verb: the conjugated verb is the second element in the sentence. The first element can be a subject, a direct object, an adverb, a prepositional phrase, a complete clause, or an interrogative word.

Transitive verbs use *haben* as their auxiliary in the present perfect tense. Notice that *haben* in each of the following sentences is the second element:

Warum *hast du seinen alten VW gekauft?*	Why have you bought his old VW?
Selbstverständlich *hat sie es nicht verstanden.*	Naturally, she hasn't understood it.
Als sie in Hamburg gewesen sind, *haben sie oft Schach gespielt.*	When they were (have been) in Hamburg, they (have) often played chess.

Verbs of motion use *sein* as their auxiliary in the present perfect tense. Notice that the position of *sein* in each of the following sentences is the second element:

Leider *ist sie wieder krank gewesen.*	Unfortunately she has been sick again.
Wie lange *ist er in der Hauptstadt geblieben?*	How long did he stay in the capital?
Vor dem Theater *sind sie einigen Touristen begegnet.*	They have encountered a few tourists in front of the theater.

It is important to remember that the past participle will be located at the end of a sentence or clause whether the conjugated verb is located before or after the subject.

The Past Perfect

The past perfect tense is identical to the present perfect tense in structure (*haben* or *sein* plus a past participle), with the past participle at the end of the sentence. The only difference is that the verb *haben* or *sein* is conjugated in the past tense. The following sentences exemplify transitive verbs in the past perfect tense. The verb *haben* is conjugated according to the person and number of the subject **and** in the past tense:

Ich hatte meinen Fahrschein **verloren***.*	I had lost my driver's license.
Hatten sie Schach **gespielt***?*	Had they played chess?

The following sentences exemplify verbs of motion in the past perfect tense. The verb **sein** is conjugated according to the person and number of the subject **and** in the past tense:

*Warst du wieder krank **gewesen**?*	Had you been sick again?
*Ihr wart mit dem Bus **gefahren**.*	You had gone by bus.

Notice in the first example above that when a sentence in the present perfect or past perfect tense is stated as a question, the sentence begins with the conjugated verb (**haben** or **sein**), but the participle still remains the last element.

When some element other than the subject begins a sentence that is in the past perfect tense, the same rule applies that applies for a present or past tense verb: the conjugated verb is the second element in the sentence. The first element can be a direct object, an adverb, a prepositional phrase, a complete clause, or an interrogative word. The past participle occurs at the end of the sentence or at the end of the clause of a compound sentence. Consider the following sentences with transitive verbs in the past perfect tense. Each one begins with some element other than the subject of the sentence:

***Den ganzen Tag** hattet ihr den Jungen zugesehen.*	You had watched the boys all day.
***Als sie in Hamburg gewesen waren**, hatten sie oft Schach gespielt.*	When they were (had been) in Hamburg, they had often played chess.

The following examples are verbs of motion in the past perfect tense. Each one begins with some element other than the subject of the sentence:

***Neulich** waren wir angekommen.*	We had recently arrived.
***Vor dem Theater** waren sie einigen Touristen begegnet.*	They had encountered a few tourists in front of the theater.

In the past perfect tense the past participle remains constant as the last element in a sentence. In compound sentences the past participle in the past perfect tense is also at the end of each clause.

*Werner hatte Bücher **gekauft**, aber sein Bruder hatte sein Geld **gespart**.*	Werner had bought books, but his brother had saved his money.

The past perfect tense tends to be used less often, particularly in the spoken language. The present perfect tense is often substituted for it.

*Ihr wart (**seid**) mit dem Bus gefahren.*
*Als sie Paris besucht hatten, waren (**sind**) sie oft ins Theater gegangen.*

The Future Tense with *werden*

The future tense can be formed by the present tense conjugation of ***werden*** followed by an infinitive at the end of the sentence. It is similar in structure and meaning to an English future tense sentence that is formed by *shall* or *will* followed by an infinitive. Look at the following future tense sentence:

*Er **wird** sich morgen die Haare **waschen**.*	He'll wash his hair tomorrow.

In the above sentence, ***waschen*** is a verb without a prefix and is irregular, but that irregularity has no effect on the tense, because ***werden*** is the conjugated verb. Likewise, the prefix on an infinitive has no influence on the tense or the word order of the sentence.

*Ich **werde** meine Freizeit im Park **verbringen**.*	I'll spend my free time in the park.
***Wirst** du **mitkommen**?*	Will you come along?

Just like other verbs, ***werden*** becomes the second element in a question that begins with an interrogative word.

*Was **wird** sie jetzt tun?*	What will she do now?

If some element other than the subject begins a future tense sentence, **werden** becomes the second element in the sentence and precedes the subject.

Das wirst du allmählich verstehen.	You will gradually understand it.
Im Winter werden wir Russisch lernen.	In the winter we're going to learn Russian.

In compound sentences the German infinitive in the future tense is at the end of each clause.

*Werner wird Bücher **kaufen**, aber sein Bruder wird sein Geld **sparen**.*	Werner will buy books, but his brother will save his money.

Remember that when **werden** stands alone in a sentence and is conjugated in any tense, it can mean *become* or *get*. Its use for the future tense occurs where there is another verb in the sentence (an infinitive) and then the meaning is *shall* or *will*.

*Meine Schwester **ist** Ärztin **geworden**.*	My sister became a doctor.
*Es **wurde** plötzlich dunkel.*	It suddenly got dark.

The English verb *get* has a variety of meanings and nuances. See the Quick-Glance Tables following Chapter 16 for a more complete look at this verb and its German equivalents.

The Future Perfect

This tense describes an action that is begun and completed in the future. It combines the conjugation of **werden** with a past participle and its appropriate auxiliary in its infinitive form (**haben** or **sein**). It is similar in structure and meaning to the English future perfect tense, which is formed by *shall* or *will* followed by *have* and the appropriate past participle. The first example is a verb that requires **haben** as its auxiliary:

*Er **wird** den Brief geschrieben haben.*	He will have written the letter.

The next example requires **sein** as the auxiliary of the participle:

*Seine Geschwister **werden** nach Hause gegangen sein.*	His brothers and sisters will have gone home.

The next two sentences are in question form. The first begins the question with the conjugated verb and ends with the participle followed by the auxiliary:

Wird *er schon abgefahren sein?*	Will he already have departed?

The second example begins with an interrogative word, thus making **werden** the second element in the sentence:

Warum **werden** *sie so früh* *zurückgekehrt sein?*	Why will they have returned so early?

If some element other than the subject begins the sentence, **werden** becomes the second element in the sentence and precedes the subject.

Bis Mittag *wird er mehr als zehn* *Stunden geschlafen haben.*	By noon he will have slept for more than ten hours.
Wenn er nach Hause kommt, *wird sie sich die Haare gewaschen* *haben.*	By the time he comes home, she'll have washed her hair.

In compound sentences the German past participle and the infinitive **haben** or **sein** are also at the end of a clause in the future perfect tense:

Werner wird Bücher **gekauft** **haben**, *aber sein Bruder wird* *sein Geld* **gespart haben**.	Werner will have bought books, but his brother will have saved his money.

When a question begins with an interrogative word (**wer**, **was**, **wo**, etc.), the conjugated verb **werden** is the second element in the sentence. Take note of these examples in the future tense:

Wirst du Klavier spielen?	Will you play the piano?
Wann *wirst du Klavier spielen?*	When will you play the piano?

Now compare the above examples with the following examples in the future perfect tense:

Wird er es geschrieben haben?	Will he have written it?
Wie wird er es geschrieben haben?	How will he have written it?

Modal Auxiliaries and *helfen, hören, lassen,* and *sehen*

The modal auxiliary verbs (*dürfen, können, mögen, müssen, sollen,* and *wollen*) and the verbs *helfen, hören, lassen,* and *sehen* in the present and past tenses are often followed by a second verbal element: **an infinitive**. The conjugated verb follows the subject and changes endings according to the person and number of the subject. The infinitive is always at the end of the sentence. And the same pattern exists in both the present and past tenses. First, let's look at some examples of modal auxiliaries in the present tense:

*Ich **darf** es nicht **sagen**.*	I may not say it.
*Du **kannst** ihm heute **helfen**.*	You can help him today.
*Es **mag sein**.*	It may be.
*Ihr **sollt** sie nicht mit dem Tabakrauch **belästigen**.*	You shouldn't annoy them with tobacco smoke.

This same word order occurs in the present tense with *helfen, hören, lassen,* and *sehen*.

*Herr Schmidt **hilft** ihnen arbeiten.*	Mr. Schmidt helps them work.
*Der Pförtner **hört** Schritte kommen.*	The doorman hears footsteps coming.
*Meine Schwester **läßt** sich die Haare **schneiden**.*	My sister gets her hair cut.
*Die Jungen **sehen** sie Fußball spielen.*	The boys see them playing soccer.

When the conjugation of the verb is in the past tense, the word order with modal auxiliaries is still the same as in the present tense.

*Ich **durfte** es nicht **tun**.*	I wasn't allowed to do it.
*Du **konntest** ein paar Sätze **schreiben**.*	You could write a couple sentences.
*Wir **mussten** zu Hause **bleiben**.*	We had to stay at home.

And the same is true of **helfen**, **hören**, **lassen**, and **sehen** in the past tense.

> *Herr Schmidt **half** ihnen*   Mr. Schmidt helped them work.
>   ***arbeiten.***
> *Meine Schwester **ließ** sich die*   My sister got her hair cut.
>   *Haare **schneiden.***

The verb **mögen** is used in the present tense to mean *like* or *may* or *might*. The past tense conjugation is **mochte**. The present and past tenses of *like* tend to be used without an infinitive at the end of the sentence and followed by a direct object.

> *Ich **mag** keine Butter.*   I don't like butter.
> *Karin **mochte** Karl einfach nicht.*   Karin simply didn't like Karl.

The use of **mag** to mean *may* or *might* is less frequent and is usually found in pat statements in the present tense.

> *Das **mag** wohl **sein**, aber ich*   That may well be, but I don't
>   *glaube es nicht.*   believe it.

There is a strong tendency to use the subjunctive conjugation **möchte**, particularly when you are saying that you not only like something but would like to have some as well. And it is this form of the verb that is used more frequently with an infinitive at the end of a sentence.

> *Ich **möchte** im Sommer nach*   In the summer I'd like to travel
>   *Europa **reisen.***   to Europe.

The modal auxiliaries indicate the **degree of obligation** to carry out the action of a verb. Refer to the Quick-Glance Tables at the end of the book for a more complete description of this concept.

The verbs **gehen** and **lernen** are also often used in the same way as the modal auxiliaries. **Gehen** and **lernen** are conjugated in either the present or past tense and are followed at the end of the sentence by an infinitive. Look at the following examples in the present tense:

*Die jungen Sportler **gehen** heute **rudern**.*	The young athletes are going rowing today.
*Ich **lerne** am See **segeln**.*	I'm learning sailing at the lake.

Compare the present tense to the following examples in the past tense. The word order is identical in both tenses:

*Viele Leute **gingen** im Park **spazieren**.*	Many people went strolling in the park.
*Er **lernte** da **schwimmen**.*	He learned to swim there.

Sentences in the future or perfect tenses with the modal auxiliaries and the verbs **helfen**, **hören**, **lassen**, **sehen**, **gehen**, and **lernen** form a double infinitive structure. This structure is a combination of two infinitives, and the second infinitive is always the modal auxiliary or one of the verbs **helfen**, **hören**, **lassen**, **sehen**, **gehen**, and **lernen**. Let's look at the future tense first:

Morgen werden wir ins Ausland reisen müssen.	We're going to have to travel overseas tomorrow.
In einigen Tagen wird er mit dem Auto nach Wien fahren dürfen.	In a few days he'll be allowed to travel to Vienna.
Sie wird sich ein neues Kleid machen lassen.	She'll have a new dress made.

Consider these examples in the present perfect tense:

Sie hat den schönen Ring nicht verkaufen wollen.	She didn't want to sell the beautiful ring.
Die Kinder haben sofort nach Hause gehen sollen.	The children were supposed to go right home after school.
Karl hat die Kinder im Park spielen sehen.	Karl saw the children playing in the park.

Just as with other verbs, the conjugated verb (**werden** or **haben**) is the second element in a statement. The double infinitive is the last element in the statement. In questions, the conjugated verb is the first element. In questions that begin with an interrogative word, the conjugated verb is the second element.

The verbs *helfen, hören, lassen, sehen, gehen,* and *lernen* can be used alone in a sentence. The same is true of modal auxiliaries. The use of all these verbs is not limited to acting as the auxiliary of an infinitive. Note the word order of these verbs when they are the only verb in a sentence:

*Sein guter Freund **hilft** ihm jeden Tag.*	His good friend helps him every day.
***Hörst** du die Musik?*	Do you hear the music?
*Er **ließ** sie im Stich.*	He left her in the lurch.
*Auf dem Dach **sieht** Frau Huber einen großen Storch.*	Mrs. Huber sees a large stork on the roof.
*Morgen **gehe** ich wieder aufs Land.*	I'm going to the country again tomorrow.
*Diese Kinder **lernen** schnell.*	These children learn fast.

The following sentences demonstrate modal auxiliaries as the only verb in a sentence. Notice that some **imply** the meaning of a missing infinitive. The meaning of that infinitive—usually *to do*—still appears in the English translation:

*Das **darfst** du nicht.*	You're not allowed to do that.
*Mein Vetter **kann** Spanisch und Russisch.*	My cousin knows Spanish and Russian.
***Mögen** Sie es nicht?*	Don't you like it?

Except for the verb *können*, which can mean *know a language*, the other modals can be used alone in a sentence elliptically. That is, the infinitive that normally would accompany the modal auxiliary is omitted and understood by context: ***Ich will es nicht (tun).*** When modal auxiliaries appear as the only verb in a sentence, they are the second element in a statement or a question beginning with an interrogative word or the first element in a question without an interrogative word.

*Man **muss** das nicht.*	One shouldn't do that.
*Was **willst** du?*	What do you want?
***Sollen** wir das nicht?*	Shouldn't we do that?

Word Order with *aber, denn, oder,* and *und*

The conjunctions **aber**, **denn**, **oder**, and **und** combine two complete sentences into a compound sentence. These conjunctions do not affect the original word order of each sentence. Look at how the following pairs of sentences combine as one. The word order in each part of a combined sentence is determined by the primary rule of word order: the conjugated verb is the second element in a statement or in a question without an interrogative word. The conjunction merely acts as a device for uniting the two sentences into one. It does not affect word order.

The first example is in the present tense, and in both clauses the conjugated verb is the second element in the sentence:

Wilhelm arbeitet in einer Fabrik. *Seine Schwester arbeitet in einem Kaufhaus.*	Wilhelm works in a factory. His sister works in a department store.
Wilhelm arbeitet in einer Fabrik, ***aber*** *seine Schwester arbeitet in einem Kaufhaus.*	Wilhelm works in a factory, but his sister works in a department store.

In the following example, the verbs are in the present tense, but the second sentence ends with an infinitive phrase. Notice that the phrase **zu tun** remains in its original position when the sentences are combined with the conjunction **denn**:

Ich habe keine Freizeit. Ich habe viel zu tun.	I have little free time. I have a lot to do.
Ich habe keine Freizeit, ***denn*** *ich habe viel zu tun.*	I have little free time because I have a lot to do.

In the following example with the modal auxiliary **können**, each clause of the combined sentence ends with the appropriate infinitive from the original sentence:

Wir können Onkel Hans besuchen. *Wir können in die Stadt fahren.*	We can visit Uncle Hans. We can drive into the city.
Wir können Onkel Hans besuchen ***oder*** *in die Stadt fahren.*	We can visit Uncle Hans or drive into the city.

The next example is in the past tense. In both clauses of the combined sentence, the conjugated verb is the second element. In the second clause the infinitive *spielen* remains at the end of the clause:

Karl spielte Klavier. Er lernte Geige spielen.	Karl played piano. He was learning to play the violin.
*Karl spielte Klavier **und** er lernte Geige spielen.*	Karl played piano, and he was learning to play the violin.

The conjunction **sondern** requires the same word order as the previous four conjunctions. However, the negative word **nicht** will be found in the first clause of the combined sentence. Here are some examples:

Sie spielt nicht nur Geige. Sie spielt auch Gitarre.	She doesn't only play the violin. She also plays the guitar.
*Sie spielt **nicht** nur Geige, **sondern** auch Gitarre.*	She doesn't only play the violin, but also the guitar.
Martin spricht nicht nur Italienisch. Er kann auch Englisch.	Martin doesn't only speak Italian. He also knows English.
*Martin spricht **nicht** nur Italienisch, **sondern** er kann auch Englisch.*	Martin not only speaks Italian, but he also knows English.

When the conjunctions **aber**, **denn**, **oder**, and **und** are used in sentences in which the tense is something other than the present or the past with a single verb, the conjugated auxiliary is the second element in the sentence and the sentence ends with either an infinitive or a past participle. Look at how the future tense is used in the two clauses combined by **aber** and **oder**:

*Ich werde nach Schweden **fahren**, aber Ilse wird nach Brasilien **fliegen**.*	I'll drive to Sweden, but Ilse will fly to Brazil.
*Wir können Schach **spielen** oder ins Kino **gehen**.*	We can play chess or go to the movies.

Notice that the past participles in the following present perfect sentences are located at the end of the clauses when the sentences are combined by **denn** and **und**:

> *Er ist zu Hause **geblieben**, denn*   He has stayed home because the
> *das Wetter ist so scheußlich*   weather has been so awful.
> ***gewesen**.*
>
> *Sie hat ihre Fahrkarte **verloren***   She lost her ticket and has gone
> *und ist zu Fuß **gegangen**.*   on foot.

Subordinating Conjunctions and Word Order

Most subordinating conjunctions introduce a clause that provides information about the time, manner, or reason of the action in the sentence. This kind of clause is called a **subordinate** or **dependent clause** because it cannot stand alone as a sentence and make complete sense. Look at the German/English example that follows. The subordinate clause shown in bold letters does not make good sense as an independent sentence:

> *Ich besuchte Tante Gerda, **als ich***   I visited Aunt Gerda when I was
> ***in Deutschland war**.*   in Germany.

The clause "when I was in Germany" has a subject ("I") and a verb ("was"), yet it makes no sense standing alone. This is a subordinate clause.

There are many subordinating conjunctions in German; see the Quick-Glance Tables following Chapter 16 for the complete list.

Each of the following sentences has a subordinate clause. The conjugated verb in the subordinate clause is correctly located at the end of the clause. The first example is in the present tense. Note that the conjugation is still appropriate for the pronoun **wir** even though the verb is located at the end of the clause:

> *Wenn wir zum Schwimmbad*   Whenever we come to the pool,
> ***kommen**, gehen wir schwimmen.*   we go swimming.

The second example uses the present tense conjugation to imply a future tense meaning. Word order has changed in the subordinate clause, but the verb is still conjugated appropriately:

Wir gehen morgen einkaufen, falls   We're going shopping tomorrow
   *wir genug Zeit **haben**.*   if we have enough time.

The same is true in the past tense. Notice that when the subordinate clause begins the sentence, the second clause has to begin with the verb, since the subordinate clause is acting as some element other than the subject.

*Als ich in Bonn **war**, **ging** ich oft*   When I was in Bonn, I often
   ins Kino.   went to the movies.
*Sobald sie die Wunde **merkte**,*   As soon as she noticed the
   ***rief** sie den Arzt an.*   wound, she phoned the doctor.

But when the subordinate clause is the second clause, the conjugated verb stands at the end of the clause. Notice that the verb in the first clause is now in the second position.

*Der Knabe **schrie** bei jedem Löffel*   The boy screamed with every
   Suppe, weil die Suppe schlecht   spoonful of soup because the
   ***schmeckte**.*   soup tasted bad.
*Mein Mann **fragte** mich immer*   My husband always asked me
   *bevor er etwas **kaufte**.*   before he bought something.

In the present perfect or past perfect tense, the conjugation of ***haben*** stands behind the participle in the subordinate clause.

*Seit er den Wagen verkauft **hat**,*   Since he sold the car, he has had
   muss er zu Fuß gehen.   to go on foot.
Nachdem Benno die Milch   After Benno had drunk his milk,
   *getrunken **hatte**, ist er ins Bett*   he went to bed.
   gegangen.
Das Schauspiel war nicht so gut,   The play wasn't as good as we
   *wie wir erwartet **hatten**.*   had expected.

If a modal auxiliary is in the subordinate clause in the present or past tense, it will be the last element in that clause.

Vater will euch helfen, soweit er   Father will help you as much as
   ***kann**.*   he can.

*Da das Wetter scheußlich **wurde**, mussten wir zu Hause bleiben.*	Since the weather turned awful, we had to stay at home.
*Ihr könnt uns besuchen sooft wie ihr Zeit **habt**.*	You can visit us as often as you have time.

As you can see from the examples above, no matter what the configuration of the verb is—a single present or past tense verb, an auxiliary (**haben** or **sein**) and a participle, or **werden** plus an infinitive in the future tense—the conjugated form of the verb is the **last** element of the subordinate clause. The same rule applies if modal auxiliaries or **helfen**, **hören**, **lassen**, **sehen**, **gehen**, or **lernen** are used in the present or past tense.

*. . . soviel wir es **verstehen**.*	. . . as much as we understand it.
*. . . soviel wir es verstehen **können**.*	. . . as much as we can understand it.
*. . . soviel wir es verstanden **haben**.*	. . . as much as we have understood it.
*. . . soviel wir es verstanden **hatten**.*	. . . as much as we had understood it.
*. . . soviel wir es verstehen **werden**.*	. . . as much as we will understand it.

Double Infinitives in Subordinate Clauses

Double infinitive structures occur in the present perfect, past perfect, future, and future perfect tenses. They occur with modal auxiliaries and with the verbs **helfen**, **hören**, **lassen**, **sehen**, **gehen**, and **lernen**. In the present and past tenses, the double infinitive does not occur:

Er muss gehorchen.	He must obey.
Ich konnte die Übersetzung nicht schreiben.	I couldn't write the translation.
Beim Militär lernten sie Arabisch sprechen und lesen.	They learned to speak and read Arabic in the army.

In the present perfect, past perfect, and future tenses, an auxiliary verb (**haben** or **werden**) is conjugated, and a double infinitive occurs at the end of the sentence. Notice the use of a double infinitive in the present perfect and past perfect tenses with ***müssen***, ***lernen***, and ***helfen***. There is no past participle in the structure:

Beim Militär haben sie Arabisch **sprechen** *und* **lesen lernen**.	They have learned to speak and read Arabic in the army.
Wir hatten dem alten Herrn **aufstehen helfen**.	We had helped the old gentleman to get up.
Er hat **gehorchen müssen**.	He has had to obey.

In the examples that follow, the future tense sentences are completed by a double infinitive just as in the present perfect and past perfect sentences. Again there is no past participle in the structure:

Ich werde die Übersetzung nicht **schreiben können**.	I will not be able to write the translation.
Wann werden Sie Ihren Wagen **reparieren lassen?**	When will you have your car repaired?

When a double infinitive occurs in a subordinate clause, which normally requires the conjugated verb to be located at the end of the sentence, the rule regarding word order is broken. The conjugated auxiliary verb (***haben*** or ***werden***) stands directly **before** the double infinitive structure. Some examples in the present perfect tense:

. . . als wir dem alten Herrn **haben** *aufstehen helfen*.	. . . when we have helped the old gentleman to get up.
. . . nachdem sie Arabisch **haben** *sprechen und lesen lernen*.	. . . after they have learned to speak and read Arabic.
. . . weil er **hat** *gehorchen müssen*.	. . . because he has had to obey.

Following are some examples of double infinitives with the future tense in subordinate clauses:

. . . ob Sie Ihren Wagen **werden** *reparieren lassen*.	. . . whether you will have your car repaired.
. . . obwohl ich die Übersetzung nicht **werde** *schreiben können*.	. . . although I will not be able to write the translation.

Exercise 1

Rewrite each sentence by starting the sentence with the word or phrase in parentheses. Beginning the sentences with an element other than the subject will change the word order. For example:

(heute) Ich bleibe zu Hause.
Heute bleibe ich zu Hause.

1. (im Februar) Wir reisen mit Verwandten nach Spanien.

   _____.

2. (nach dem Krieg) Die Flüchtlinge kamen langsam nach Hause.

   _____.

3. (als Onkel Peter zu Besuch kam) Vater kaufte ein neues Bett.

   _____.

4. (später) Herr Doktor Schmidt ging zum Krankenhaus zurück.

   _____.

5. (schnell) Der weinende Junge lief ins Wohnzimmer.

   _____.

Exercise 2

Rewrite each sentence by beginning it with the element underlined. Make the appropriate change in the word order.

1. Karl war den ganzen Tag in der Stadt.

   _____.

2. Die Kinder spielen Schach.

   _____.

3. Ich fahre <u>nächste Woche</u> in die Schweiz.

_____.

4. Er besuchte eine Freundin, <u>als er in Hamburg war</u>.

_____.

5. Wir gehen <u>morgen</u> wieder in die Schule.

_____.

Exercise 3

Rewrite the following sentences in the present perfect tense and in the past perfect tense. Place the verbal elements in the appropriate position.

1. Wen verhaftet die Polizei?

_____.

_____.

2. Am Abend kommt Herr Schneider von der Arbeit nach Hause.

_____.

_____.

3. Als Klaudia in der Bäckerei war, begegnete sie Herrn Kraus.

_____.

_____.

Exercise 4

Rewrite each sentence with the modal auxiliary in parentheses. Keep the same tense.

1. (wollen) Die alten Leute spazieren im Garten.

_____.

2. (müssen) Ich arbeitete bis in die Nacht.

_____.

3. (können) Frau Brenner rechtfertigt ihre Meinung nicht.

_____.

4. (sollen) Sie hat ihre Hausarbeit getan.

_____.

Exercise 5

Rewrite each sentence by beginning it with the phrase *Ich wusste nicht,
dass.* . . . For example:

Sie kennen meine Kusine.
Ich wusste nicht, dass Sie meine Kusine kennen.

1. Er hat den Wecker reparieren lassen.

_____.

2. Du bist mit dem letzten Zug gekommen.

_____.

3. Die alte Dame hat den Dieb weglaufen sehen.

_____.

4. Die Kinder haben großen Hunger gehabt.

_____.

5. Sie hat einen neuen Computer kaufen wollen.

_____.

Exercise 6

Complete each sentence with any appropriate phrase.

1. Meine Kusine wohnt in Tschechien, und ——————.

2. Die Zwillinge sind zehn Jahre alt, aber ——————.

3. Er hat sein Gepäck verloren, während ——————.

4. Franziska ist noch im Bett, weil ——————.

5. Der Roman ist nicht interessant, sondern ——————.

Dative Verbs

Indirect objects require the dative case in German. They are the element in a sentence that answers *to whom* or *for whom*.

*Ich gebe **der armen Frau** ein Brot.*	I give the poor woman a loaf of bread.
*Karl schickte **ihm** die Bücher.*	Karl sent him the books.

There are other instances when the dative case is required because the verb in the sentence is a **dative verb**. However, the object in such a sentence is not an indirect object.

The dative object of a dative verb sometimes causes confusion for English speakers. Translated into English, the dative object often becomes a direct object. For that reason, there is a tendency for English speakers to employ the accusative case where the dative case is needed. Therefore, it is important to distinguish the German dative verbs and to use the dative case appropriately. Compare the German dative objects and the English direct objects:

*Ich glaube **dir**.*	I believe **you**.
*Er dient **der Frau**.*	He serves **the woman**.
*Sie sehen **den Kindern** zu.*	They watch **the children**.

You will find a list of commonly used dative verbs in the Quick-Glance Tables at the end of this book. There are numerous dative verbs, and you can easily determine which German verbs are dative because most dictionaries list verbs together with the case they require. An entry will look something like this:

helfen, *ir.v.n.* (*aux.* haben) (*Dative*) help

Dative verbs can be used in any tense or with any of the modal auxiliaries. The object of a dative verb will always be in the dative case. The tense of the verb has no effect on the case of the object, as you will see in the following examples.

The verb *glauben* is shown in the present and past tense. In both instances the object of the verb is in the dative case:

Glaubst du mir?	Do you believe me?
Glaubtest du ihm?	Did you believe him?

The verb *helfen* is shown in the present perfect and past perfect tense. In both instances the object of the verb is in the dative case:

Hast du ihr geholfen?	Have you helped her?
Hattest du ihnen geholfen?	Had you helped them?

The verb *danken* is shown in the future tense. The object of the verb is in the dative case:

Wirst du ihm danken?	Will you thank him?

Impersonal Expressions

In addition to the dative verbs, there are a few impersonal verbal expressions that often begin with the pronoun *es* and that require the use of the dative case.

es fällt Ihnen ein	it occurs to you
es gefällt dem Mann	the man likes it
es geht dem Kind gut	the child feels well
es gelingt mir	I succeed, I manage to do something
es genügt der Dame	the lady's satisfied with something
es glückt dir	you prosper, you succeed
es kommt mir darauf an	it seems to me
es kommt mir vor	it appears to me
es passt mir gut	it suits me fine
es scheint ihr	it seems to her
es schmeckt ihm	it tastes good to him

| *es sitzt ihm gut* | it fits him well |
| *es steht ihr gut* | she looks good in it |

The impersonal expressions are not used exclusively with the pronoun *es*. Most any singular or plural noun that makes sense in the sentence can be used as the subject of these verbs.

| *Dieses Theaterstück hat uns sehr gut gefallen.* | We liked this play a lot. |
| *Diese schwarzen Kleider passen Ihnen nicht gut.* | These black dresses just don't suit you. |

These expressions cannot always be translated word for word into English. You must know two things: (1) the German usage of the expression and (2) what it means in English. Compare the following impersonal expressions in German with their English meaning:

Es gelang ihm nicht das Problem zu lösen.	He didn't succeed in solving the problem.
Es gelingt dem Studenten nicht, seine Dissertation rechtzeitig zu beendigen.	The student fails to finish his dissertation on time.
Es fiel mir ein, dass ich meine Brille verloren hatte.	It occurred to me that I had lost my glasses.

The object of a dative impersonal expression will always be in the dative case. The tense of the verb has no effect on the case of the object, as you will note in the examples that follow.

The expression *es geht* is shown in the present and past tense. In both instances the object of the verb is in the dative case:

| *Es geht ihm besser.* | He feels better. |
| *Es ging ihm besser.* | He felt better. |

The expression *es passt* is shown in the present perfect and past perfect tense. In both instances the object of the verb is in the dative case:

| *Es hat ihm nicht gepasst.* | It hasn't suited him. |
| *Es hatte ihm nicht gepasst.* | It hadn't suited him. |

The expression *es gefällt* is shown in the future tense. The object of the verb is in the dative case:

Es wird euch gefallen.   You will like it.

Dative Verbs with Modal Auxiliaries

No matter the tense or the other verb forms used in a sentence (for example, participle or infinitive), a dative verb or impersonal expression will still require a dative object. When modal auxiliaries are used with dative verbs they also require a dative object. In such constructions the modal auxiliaries are the conjugated verbs, not the dative verbs, as you will see in the following examples.

The modals *können* and *sollen* are shown in the present tense with a dative verb. In both instances the object of the verb is in the dative case.

Ich kann dir einfach nicht glauben.   I simply can't believe you.
Wir sollen dem Reiseleiter folgen.   We should follow the tour guide.

The modal *müssen* is shown in the past tense with a dative verb. The object of the verb is in the dative case:

Karin musste ihren Eltern damit   Karin had to help her parents
    helfen.   with it.

The modal *wollen* is shown in the present perfect tense with a dative verb. The object of the verb is in the dative case:

Wem haben Sie es sagen wollen?   To whom have you wanted to
                                        tell it?

The modal *wollen* is shown in the future tense with a dative verb. The object of the verb is in the dative case:

Er wird der Königin nicht dienen   He won't want to serve the
    wollen.   queen.

Exercise 1

Fill in the blank with the dative form of the word or phrase in parentheses.

1. (der Lehrer) Der Schüler hat _____ sofort

    geantwortet.

2. (das kleine Kind) Die Mutter drohte _____

    mit dem Finger.

3. (ich) Es scheint _____ , dass du wieder

    krank bist.

4. (seine Tante) Er dankte _____ für das

    Geschenk.

5. (er) Das Konzert hat _____ sehr imponiert.

Exercise 2

Rewrite each sentence in the present perfect tense.

1. Der Alkohol schadet dem Gehirn.

    _____ .

2. Ein gutes Wörterbuch kann einem Studenten nützen.

    _____ .

3. Der lange Zug hatte sich dem Hauptbahnhof genähert.

    _____ .

4. Die Hunde wollen dem Herrn überall folgen.

    _____ .

5. Der rote Apfel schmeckte dem lächelnden Jungen sehr gut.

_____.

Exercise 3

Using the sentence elements in parentheses, write pairs of similar sentences. Use a dative verb in the first and a transitive verb in the second. For example:

(er/helfen/sehen/Frau)
Er hilft der Frau.
Er sieht die Frau.

1. (wir/danken/besuchen/unsere neuen Freunde)

_____.

_____.

2. (der Kellner/dienen/beschreiben/die unhöflichen Kunden)

_____.

_____.

3. (ich/imponieren/enttäuschen/mein Professor)

_____.

_____.

4. (der alte Hund/folgen/finden/der fremde Mann)

_____.

_____.

Accusative Reflexive Verbs

Reflexive verbs are those that are used together with a reflexive pronoun. The function of a reflexive verb is to *reflect* the action of the verb from the subject to the direct object. Take note of the following examples in English:

> John hurts himself. (John hurts **John**.)
> Mary prides herself on her looks. (Mary prides **Mary** on her looks.)

If a pronoun object is not the same gender and number as the subject, the object pronoun can be any personal pronoun. But if the pronoun object and the subject are the same gender and number, then a reflexive pronoun is used. Compare the following pairs of sentences:

DIFFERENT NUMBER OR GENDER	SAME NUMBER AND GENDER
I carry him far.	I carry myself well.
You enjoy it.	You enjoy yourself.

German does very much the same thing. But in German you must also distinguish between accusative and dative reflexive verbs.

The accusative reflexive of a verb most often takes the place of a direct object. The reflexive pronouns look, for the most part, like the accusative personal pronouns: *ich—mich, du—dich, wir—uns,* and *ihr—euch.* The exception is the third person singular and plural: *er—sich, sie* (*s.*)—*sich, es—sich, Sie—sich,* and *sie* (*pl.*)—*sich.*

The reflexive pronouns are only used with their nominative counterparts (*ich—mich, er—sich, wir—uns,* etc.). Look at the difference in meaning between the use of an accusative personal pronoun in a sentence followed by one with an accusative reflexive pronoun in these examples:

*Er ärgert **ihn**.*	He annoys him (someone else).
*Er ärgert **sich**.*	He is annoyed. (He annoys himself.)
*Sie haben **uns** überzeugt.*	They convinced us (someone else).
*Sie haben **sich** überzeugt.*	They convinced themselves.
*Ich wasche **es**.*	I wash it (something else).
*Ich wasche **mich**.*	I wash myself.

Naturally, an accusative reflexive pronoun can replace a direct object that is a noun:

*Wie kann ich **die Situation** ändern?*	How can I change the situation?
*Wie kann ich **mich** ändern?*	How can I change myself?
*Wir waschen **den schmutzigen Hund**.*	We wash the dirty dog.
*Wir waschen **uns**.*	We wash ourselves.

The change of tense in no way affects the choice of a reflexive pronoun. The reflexive pronoun in each sentence is the **counterpart** of the personal pronoun subject, and it is positioned in the sentence after the conjugated verb **no matter what the tense of the verb is**.

Ich wasche mich.	I wash myself.
Ich wusch mich.	I washed myself.
Ich habe mich gewaschen.	I have washed myself.
Ich werde mich waschen.	I will wash myself.
Du benimmst dich schlecht.	You behave badly.
Du benahmst dich schlecht.	You behaved badly.
Du hast dich schlecht benommen.	You have behaved badly.
Du wirst dich schlecht benehmen.	You will behave badly.

In the above two sets of examples, the verbs had an irregular conjugation. The following two verbs have a regular conjugation. The kind of conjugation a verb has does not affect the use of a reflexive pronoun:

Er beeilt sich.	He hurries.
Er hat sich beeilt.	He has hurried.
Wir freuen uns.	We are glad.
Wir haben uns gefreut.	We were glad.

All reflexive verbs use **haben** as their auxiliary in the present perfect, past perfect, and future perfect tenses:

Ihr habt euch geirrt.	You have been mistaken.
Ihr hattet euch geirrt.	You had been mistaken.
Ihr werdet euch geirrt haben.	You will have been mistaken.
Sie haben sich gesetzt.	They have sat down.
Sie hatten sich gesetzt.	They had sat down.
Sie werden sich gesetzt haben.	They will have sat down.

In the case of the interrogative pronouns **wer** and **was**, the third person singular **sich** is always the reflexive form:

Wer zieht sich an?	Who is dressing?
Wer zog sich an?	Who dressed?
Wer hat sich angezogen?	Who has dressed?
Wer wird sich anziehen?	Who will dress?
Was bewegt sich?	What is moving?
Was bewegte sich?	What was moving?
Was hat sich bewegt?	What has moved?
Was wird sich bewegen?	What will move?

All nouns that are in the third person, whether singular or plural, use **sich** as their reflexive form:

Die Kinder benehmen sich gut.	The children behave well.
Das Kind hat sich erkältet.	The child caught a cold.

Many accusative reflexive verbs do not use the reflexive pronoun as a substitute for a direct object:

DIRECT OBJECT	ACCUSATIVE REFLEXIVE
Er ärgert ihn.	*Er ärgert sich.*

Instead, they are verbs that use a reflexive as part of the whole meaning of the verb. Therefore, the English translation often shows no reflexive form at all, as in the following examples:

Ich habe mich erkältet.	I caught a cold.
Er benimmt sich sehr schlecht.	He behaves very badly.
Erinnerst du dich daran?	Do you remember that?
Sie irren sich.	You're wrong.

The accusative reflexive is sometimes used to reflect a passive voice meaning:

Es wird sich an dieser Ecke befinden.	It will be located on this corner.
Hans interessierte sich dafür.	Hans was interested in it.

Reflexive verbs in their infinitive form are always shown with the third person reflexive pronoun **sich**: **sich erinnern**, **sich freuen**, and so on. However, a dictionary entry will sometimes look like this:

erkälten, 1. *v.a.* cool, chill. 2. *v.r.* catch cold.

The letters *v.a.* tell you that the meaning of the **active verb** is *cool, chill.* The letters *v.r.* tell you that the meaning of the **reflexive verb** is *catch cold.* The infinitive of the reflexive verb would be **sich erkälten**.

You will find a list of commonly used reflexive verbs in the Quick-Glance Tables at the end of the book.

Exercise 1

Rewrite the following sentences and change the direct object in bold print to the appropriate reflexive pronoun.

1. Du hast **einen neuen Pullover** angezogen.

_____ .

2. Sie erinnert **ihren Mann** an ihren Hochzeitstag.

_____.

3. Wie könnt ihr **es** ändern?

_____.

4. Ich frage **ihn**, ob wir genug gespart haben.

_____.

5. Haben Sie **die Nachbarn** wieder geärgert?

_____.

Exercise 2

Write original sentences with the reflexive verbs in parentheses.

1. (sich irren)

_____.

2. (sich waschen)

_____.

3. (sich beeilen)

_____.

4. (sich ausziehen)

_____.

5. (sich fragen)

_____.

5

Dative Reflexive Pronouns

Just as accusative reflexive pronouns can replace a direct object, a dative reflexive pronoun can replace an indirect object or be the object of a dative verb. The dative reflexive pronouns look, for the most part, like the dative personal pronouns: *ich—mir*, *du—dir*, *wir—uns*, and *ihr—euch*. The exception is the third person singular and plural: *er—sich*, *sie* (*s.*)—*sich*, *es—sich*, *Sie—sich*, and *sie* (*pl.*)—*sich*. Take note that the third person dative and accusative reflexive pronouns are identical.

The interrogatives *wer* and *was* as well as all singular or plural third person nouns use *sich* as their dative reflexive pronoun.

Just as accusative reflexive pronouns can replace an accusative pronoun or noun, dative reflexive pronouns can replace dative pronouns or nouns. Look at the difference in meaning between using a dative personal pronoun and using a dative reflexive pronoun in these examples:

*Sie kaufen **ihm** eine neue Brille.*	You buy him new glasses (someone else).
*Sie kaufen **sich** eine neue Brille.*	You buy yourself new glasses.
*Ich bestellte **dir** ein Glas Bier.*	I ordered you a glass of beer (someone else).
*Ich bestellte **mir** ein Glas Bier.*	I ordered myself a glass of beer.

Now compare the dative noun with the dative reflexive pronoun in the sentences that follow. These sentences require dative objects because they are objects of dative verbs:

*Ich verzeihe **dem Mann** diese Dummheit nicht.*	I don't pardon the man for this stupidity (someone else).

*Ich verzeihe **mir** diese Dummheit nicht.*	I don't excuse myself for this stupidity.
*Du hilfst **den Leuten**, so gut du kannst.*	You help the people as well as you can (someone else).
*Du hilfst **dir**, so gut du kannst.*	You help yourself as well as you can.

English and German are similar in that they can both substitute a reflexive pronoun for an object in a sentence. In German, of course, you have to consider whether the object is accusative or dative.

German sometimes uses a dative reflexive where English would use a possessive pronoun. The implication of such a structure is that something **personal** is being undertaken.

If you say that you're washing your hands and you use the word *hands* as a direct object in German, the sentence sounds quite strange and imparts the meaning that your hands have been removed from your arms and you are washing them in a sink of soapy water. In German, the dative reflexive is required instead. Compare the following three pairs of example sentences. The first in each pair shows an inanimate direct object in the accusative case; the second illustrates a dative reflexive pronoun for a "personal" activity.

Ich wasche die Teller.	I wash the plates.
*Ich wasche **mir** die Hände.*	I wash my hands.
Karl hat den Wecker gebrochen.	Karl broke the alarm clock.
*Karl hat **sich** den Finger gebrochen.*	Karl broke his finger.
Du putzt den Boden.	You clean the floor.
*Du putzt **dir** die Zähne.*	You brush your teeth.

Notice that German possessive adjectives in these personal expressions are avoided and articles are used in place of them. Other expressions that say you are doing something of a personal nature will follow the same pattern.

Wir kämmen uns die Haare.	We comb our hair.
Ich ziehe mir einen Pullover an.	I put on a sweater.

The verbs that have to do with getting dressed require a special "look." Three high-frequency verbs are derived from the infinitive **ziehen** and restated with prefixes. The prefixes change the meaning of the verb.

anziehen	to put on (clothes)
ausziehen	to take off (clothes)
umziehen	to change (clothes)

These three verbs can be used with a direct object. The meaning is that someone is putting on, taking off, or changing certain apparel.

Ich möchte den neuen Regenmantel anziehen.	I'd like to put on my new raincoat.
Die nassen Kinder zogen ihre Hemden aus.	The wet children took off their shirts.
Der schwitzende Läufer zieht die Schuhe um.	The sweating runner changes shoes.

The same verbs can also be used with an accusative reflexive pronoun. In that case the meaning deals with dressing in general and has no particular article of clothing specified.

Nach einer langen Dusche habe ich mich angezogen.	After a long shower I got dressed.
Der schüchterne Junge will sich nicht ausziehen.	The shy boy doesn't want to undress.
Kannst du dich nicht schneller umziehen?	Can't you change faster?

Finally, these verbs can be used with an indirect object that is in the form of a dative reflexive pronoun. In addition, the sentence will also contain a direct object (an article of clothing).

Sie möchte sich ein blaues Kleid anziehen.	She'd like to put on a blue dress.
Willst du dir den schweren Mantel ausziehen?	Do you want to take off your heavy coat?
Er hat sich die Stiefel umziehen wollen.	He wanted to change his boots.

These examples with the verb *ziehen* exemplify a **personal** action being undertaken similar to the ones mentioned earlier (e.g., *Ich wasche mir die Hände*).

You will find a list of commonly used reflexive verbs in the Quick-Glance Tables at the end of the book.

Exercise 1
Fill in the blank with the appropriate dative reflexive pronoun.

1. Klaudia möchte _____ einen neuen Wagen kaufen.

2. Meine Schwestern haben _____ die schönen Röcke angezogen.

3. Wo kann ich _____ die Hände waschen?

4. Kannst du _____ nicht verzeihen?

5. Dürfen wir _____ ein Stück Kuchen nehmen?

Exercise 2
Write a sentence with each of the verbs in parentheses. Use the article of apparel specified. Do not use a reflexive.

1. (anziehen) eine alte Jacke

_____.

2. (ausziehen) die gelbe Bluse

_____.

3. (umziehen) meine Schuhe

_____.

Exercise 3

Write a sentence with each of the accusative reflexive verb phrases. Do not include an article of apparel.

1. (sich anziehen wollen)

_____.

2. (sich ausziehen)

_____.

3. (sich umziehen müssen)

_____.

Exercise 4

Write a sentence with each of the dative reflexive verb phrases. Include the article of apparel provided.

1. (sich anziehen) die warmen Handschuhe

_____.

2. (sich ausziehen) der lange Rock

_____.

3. (sich umziehen) die Stiefel

_____.

Exercise 5

Rewrite each sentence by changing the phrase in bold print to the appropriate dative reflexive pronoun.

1. Martin widerspricht **seiner Mutter**.

_____.

2. Kannst du **deinem Bruder** nicht verzeihen?

_____.

3. Tante Luise hat **ihrer Tochter** einen Pelzmantel gekauft.

_____.

4. Sie helfen **Ihren Nachbarn**, so gut Sie können.

_____.

5. Ich habe **dem Kind** die Schuhe ausgezogen.

_____.

6. Kinder, habt ihr **den Kleinen** die Haare gekämmt?

_____.

Inseparable Prefixes

Many languages use prefixes to change the meaning of a verb. In English there are many old words in the language—Anglo-Saxon words—that use prefixes much the same way as they are used in German. And just as in German, a verb with a prefix derives a completely new meaning, as in the following examples:

bid—forbid
go—forego
have—behave
head—behead

English gets much of its vocabulary from foreign sources, and one of its greatest contributors is Latin. Numerous Latin words are changed by prefixes, and these words exist in English as well. But the meanings of the Latin prefixes escape the English speaker, and the words are, for the most part, accepted as individual concepts. Consider the following:

fluent—confluence—influence
pending—depend—expend

German uses prefixes in the same way. But in many cases, the prefixes have a meaning that helps the German speaker to flavor his or her speech with just the nuance of meaning that is desired. Consider the English word *excite*. If you look the word up in a dictionary, you will find more than one entry for it. That's because there are nuances of meaning to *excite*, and they are expressed in German by prefixes added to the stem *-reg*.

aufregen	excite, rouse, incite
erregen	excite, stir up, stimulate
regen	excite, move, stir, animate

Understanding German prefixes well will give you a greater comprehension of what is expressed in both speech and writing and will make you a more effective user of the language.

In German there are eight basic inseparable prefixes: **be-**, **emp-**, **ent-**, **er-**, **ge-**, **miss-**, **ver-**, and **zer-**. They are called **inseparable**: they never separate from the stem of a verb no matter what the tense is. Inseparable prefixes are easily identified because they are never the stressed syllable of the verb. The stress is always on the stem of the verb:

*be**klag**en*	to complain
*emp**fehl**en*	to recommend
*ent**komm**en*	to escape
*er**wart**en*	to expect
*ge**hör**en*	to belong
*miss**trau**en*	to mistrust
*ver**steh**en*	to understand
*zer**stör**en*	to destroy

In addition to the eight basic inseparable prefixes there are eight others that are **primarily** separable prefixes but are used in some instances as inseparable prefixes: **durch-**, **hinter-**, **über-**, **um-**, **unter-**, **voll-**, **wider-**, and **wieder-**. When they are used as inseparable prefixes, the stress is never on the prefix. The stress is on the stem of the verb. Following are some example verbs:

*durch**dring**en*	to penetrate
*hinter**bleib**en*	to remain behind
*über**rasch**en*	to surprise
*um**arm**en*	to embrace
*unter**brech**en*	to interrupt
*voll**end**en*	to complete
*wider**sprech**en*	to contradict
*wieder**hol**en*	to repeat

Note that *hinter-* as a separable prefix is primarily found in regional or colloquial expressions and that *wiederholen* is the only verb where *wieder-* is used as an inseparable prefix.

Verbs that have inseparable prefixes are, for the most part, conjugated like other verbs. Conjugations in the present, past, and future are formed in the same manner as with verbs that have no prefix. The only difference occurs with the past participle of the present perfect tense, past perfect tense, and future perfect tense. In those tenses a *ge-* prefix is not added to the participle because the inseparable prefix cannot separate from the verb, making the participial prefix *ge-* unnecessary. Compare, for example, the present and past perfect tense of *lernen* and *verlernen*:

er hat gelernt, er hatte gelernt   *er hat verlernt, er hatte verlernt*

The **ge-** prefix is omitted when there is an inseparable prefix on the verb. This is true whether the verb is regular or irregular. Compare the present and past perfect of the irregular verbs *sprechen* and *besprechen*:

er hat gesprochen, er hatte   *er hat besprochen, er hatte*
gesprochen   *besprochen*

When an inseparable prefix is attached to a verb, it has no influence on whether the verb follows a regular or an irregular conjugational pattern. However, in the present perfect, past perfect, and future perfect tense, the choice of *haben* or *sein* as the auxiliary is often dependent upon the prefix used. Consider the following examples; one has a regular verb, and the other has an irregular verb, but both verbs use *haben* as their auxiliary:

sie verhungern	they starve to death
sie haben verhungert	they have starved to death
sie hatten verhungert	they had starved to death
sie werden verhungert haben	they will have starved to death
es gefällt mir	I like it
es hat mir gefallen	I have liked it
es hatte mir gefallen	I had liked it
es wird mir gefallen haben	I will have liked it

Compare those two verbs to the following two verbs. One is regular and the other is irregular, but both use *sein* as their auxiliary:

wir verreisen	we go on a journey
wir sind verreist	we have gone on a journey
wir waren verreist	we had gone on a journey
wir werden verreist sein	we will have gone on a journey
ich entkomme	I escape
ich bin entkommen	I have escaped
ich war entkommen	I had escaped
ich werde entkommen sein	I will have escaped

The auxiliary of the verb is determined by meaning and usage, that is, whether the verb is transitive or intransitive or has some special application which requires a particular auxiliary. Compare the following:

Er ist gefallen.	He has fallen.
Es hat mir gefallen.	I liked it.

When *fallen* means *to fall*, it is a verb of motion and requires *sein* as its auxiliary. But the prefix *ge-* changes the verb to a transitive verb *gefallen*, which now means *to be pleasing* and requires *haben* as its auxiliary. The two participles look identical but have different meanings and therefore use different auxiliaries. The verb *gefallen* means *to be pleasing* but is used most often where English says *to like*:

Der Hut gefällt mir.	The hat is pleasing to me. (I like the hat.)

Some of the inseparable prefixes have a specific grammatical function. Others change the meaning of the stem verb in an identifiable manner. Let's look at some of the prefixes and the clues they give to their usage.

Certain prefixes indicate that a verb is transitive. The most common of these is the inseparable prefix *be-*. This prefix is **usually** an indicator that there should be a direct object in the sentence. Notice the addition of the direct object in these example sentences:

*Die amerikanischen Touristen besichtigen **die Stadt**.*	The American tourists are going sightseeing in the city.

*Warum musst du **dich** immer beklagen?*	Why do you always have to complain?
*Wer hat **die letzte Frage** beantwortet?*	Who answered the last question?

When attached to an intransitive verb of motion, the prefix ***be-*** changes that verb to a transitive verb that takes a direct object. And the meaning of the newly formed verb is also altered. Notice what happens to the perfect tense conjugations when the prefix ***be-*** is added to the verb ***kommen***:

Ich komme nach Hause.	I come home.
*Ich **bin** nach Hause gekommen.*	I have come home.
*Ich **war** nach Hause gekommen.*	I had come home.
*Ich **be**komme einen Brief.*	I receive a letter.
*Ich **habe** einen Brief **be**kommen.*	I have received a letter.
*Ich **hatte** einen Brief **be**kommen.*	I had received a letter.

The verb of motion ***kommen*** became a transitive verb by the addition of the prefix ***be-***. In the next examples, the verb of motion ***gehen*** makes the same transformation:

Er geht schnell.	He goes fast.
*Er **ist** schnell gegangen.*	He has gone fast.
*Er **war** schnell gegangen.*	He had gone fast.
*Er **be**geht eine Sünde.*	He commits a sin.
*Er **hat** eine Sünde **be**gangen.*	He has committed a sin.
*Er **hatte** eine Sünde **be**gangen.*	He had committed a sin.

An important exception to the use of the prefix ***be-*** as an indicator that there should be a direct object in the sentence is the verb ***begegnen***. This is a dative verb and requires ***sein*** as its auxiliary:

*Karl **ist** dem Professor nach der Vorlesung begegnet.*	Karl encountered the professor after the lecture.
*Da **sind** wir zwei Ausländern begegnet.*	We encountered two foreigners there.

The prefix *emp-* is a mutation of the prefix *ent-*. If you check your dictionary, you will find that there are only three verbs that use the prefix *emp-*: **empfangen** (*to receive*), **empfehlen** (*to recommend*), and **empfinden** (*to perceive*). However, there is also the casual form of **empfinden**: it is the verb **empfindeln** and it means *to be sentimental*.

The prefix *ent-* is used with many verbs of motion. It implies the idea of escaping, absconding with something, or removing something. The object of such a verb is often in the dative case.

Wie kann er dem Dieb entfliehen?	How can he escape the thief?
Jemand hat mir die Tasche entrissen.	Someone grabbed away my purse.
Der Herzog wurde enthauptet.	The duke was beheaded.

The prefix *er-* is used in a variety of contexts, but one of the clearest is the idea of an action resulting in death.

erschießen	to shoot
ertrinken	to drown
erwürgen	to strangle

The prefix *miss-* usually indicates that something has been done wrongly.

missbrauchen	to misuse
misshandeln	to treat wrongly

Similarly, the prefix *ver-* also sometimes suggests that something has been done wrongly or with a negative result.

verlernen	to unlearn, forget
verstimmen	to put in a bad mood

Note that this prefix induces other new meanings as well:

verbessern	to improve, correct
verlieren	to lose

Although **ver-** can give clues to the meaning of a verb, it is wise not to guess at verbs with this prefix but to look them up in a dictionary.

Finally, the prefix *zer-* is the last one that provides a verb with a new meaning that can be easily understood. It implies that something has gone to pieces or bits or to a nonsolid state.

zergehen	to melt, liquefy
zerreißen	to rip to shreds

Other prefixes also modify the meaning of a verb. But they are not always a clear indicator of what the new meaning of the verb should be. Therefore, it is good advice to rely on a dictionary to help you discover the precise meaning of a verb with an inseparable prefix. Prefixes can steer you in the right direction of a verb's meaning or can give you the gist of what is meant, but for accuracy turn to a dictionary.

Exercise 1

Complete each sentence with the appropriate form of the verb provided in parentheses.

1. (durchweben) Der Stoff ist mit Blumen _____ .

2. (erleichtern) Wie können wir dir die Arbeit _____ ?

3. (bekommen) Gestern _____ ich ein Geschenk von Oma.

4. (verlängern) Warum haben Sie Ihre Dissertation _____ ?

5. (unterbrechen) Er hat schon wieder unser Gespräch _____ .

Exercise 2
Rewrite each of the following sentences in the present perfect tense.

1. Die Kinder verstehen das neue Wort.

_____.

2. Niemand besucht Onkel Heinz.

_____.

3. Die Soldaten zerstören das Dorf.

_____.

4. Es gelingt mir nicht.

_____.

5. Die Katzen entlaufen dem kleinen Mädchen.

_____.

Exercise 3
Write original sentences with the verbs in parentheses: one sentence with
the verb without a prefix and one sentence with the verb with a prefix.

1. (warten/erwarten)

_____.

_____.

2. (kommen/bekommen)

_____.

_____.

3. (laufen/entlaufen)

_____ .

_____ .

4. (stehen/entstehen)

_____ .

_____ .

5. (schreiben/beschreiben)

_____ .

_____ .

Separable Prefixes

Although both English and German have inseparable prefixes, English does not have a category of separable prefixes like German does. Therefore, it is important to take a close look at German separable prefixes.

German separable prefixes are composed of prepositions and adverbs. This means that their list is quite long. A separable prefix is identified by the location of the stress **on the separable prefix** attached to a verb.

You have already encountered certain prefixes that can be separable or inseparable. Their function as separable or inseparable can be distinguished by the location of the stress on the verb. These prefixes are *durch-*, *hinter-*, *über-*, *um-*, *unter-*, *voll-*, *wider-*, and *wieder-*. Notice how the location of the stress determines the kind of prefix that is attached to the verb. The verbs listed on the left have an inseparable prefix. The stress is on the stem of these verbs. The verbs listed on the right have a separable prefix. The stress is on the prefix of these verbs.

*durch**web**en*	to interweave	*durchlesen*	to read through
*hinter**lassen***	to leave behind	N/A	
*über**setzen***	to translate	*über**fahren***	to cross over (by vehicle)
*um**arm**en*	to embrace	*um**bringen***	to kill
*unter**drücken***	to suppress	*unter**kommen***	to find refuge
*voll**end**en*	to complete	*voll**füllen***	to fill up
*wider**sprechen***	to contradict	*wider**spiegeln***	to reflect
*wieder**hol**en*	to repeat	*wieder**holen***	to fetch, bring back

Take special note of the verb *wieder**holen***. Depending upon the stress, it can be a verb with a separable or an inseparable prefix. And dependent upon the kind of prefix **wieder-** is, the meaning of the verb is radically different.

*Der Ausländer wieder**holte** den langen Satz.*	The foreigner repeated the long sentence.
*Der kleine Hund holte den Ball **wieder**.*	The little dog brought the ball back.

Now compare two similar sentences in all the tenses with the verb **wieder<u>holen</u>**, which has the stress on the stem, and with the verb **<u>wieder</u>holen**, which has the stress on the separable prefix. Notice that the **separable prefix** separates from the stem of the verb in the present and past tenses and is separated from the participle by the prefix **ge-** in the perfect tenses.

Er wiederholt den Satz.	He repeats the sentence.
Er wiederholte den Satz.	He repeated the sentence.
Er hat den Satz wiederholt.	He has repeated the sentence.
Er hatte den Satz wiederholt.	He had repeated the sentence.
Er wird den Satz wiederholen.	He will repeat the sentence.
Er wird den Satz wiederholt haben.	He will have repeated the sentence.

Er holt den Ball wieder.	He brings the ball back.
Er holte den Ball wieder.	He brought the ball back.
*Er hat den Ball wieder**ge**holt.*	He has brought the ball back.
*Er hatte den Ball wieder**ge**holt.*	He had brought the ball back.
Er wird den Ball wiederholen.	He will bring the ball back.
*Er wird den Ball wieder**ge**holt haben.*	He will have brought the ball back.

Hinter- as a separable prefix is primarily found in regional dialects. And **wiederholen** is the only verb where **wieder-** is used as an inseparable prefix.

Remember that there are innumerable verbs that can use the same prefix. In general, a prefix changes the meaning of similar verbs in the same way. For example, most verbs of motion that have the prefix **an-** usually derive the meaning *to arrive*. But other changes in meaning caused by a separable prefix are not always constant. The best advice is to check verbs with prefixes in a dictionary. Notice how the prefix **ab-** changes the meaning of the following verbs:

fahren	to drive	*abfahren*	to depart
spielen	to play	*abspielen*	to take place
stellen	to put	*abstellen*	to put away

The prefix **zu-** changes the meaning of verbs in yet another way:

machen	to make	*zumachen*	to close
nehmen	to take	*zunehmen*	to increase
schlagen	to beat	*zuschlagen*	to slam shut

All verbs with a separable prefix place the prefix at the end of the sentence in the present and past tenses. And they all separate the prefix from the participle by the prefix **ge-** in the perfect tenses. Look at these examples of one regular and one irregular verb:

*Sie redet mich **an**.*	She addresses me.
*Sie redete mich **an**.*	She addressed me.
*Sie hat mich **an**geredet.*	She has addressed me.
*Sie hatte mich **an**geredet.*	She had addressed me.
*Sie wird mich **an**reden.*	She will address me.
*Sie wird mich **an**geredet haben.*	She will have addressed me.
*Wir kommen um 7 Uhr **an**.*	We arrive at seven o'clock.
*Wir kamen um 7 Uhr **an**.*	We arrived at seven o'clock.
*Wir sind um 7 Uhr **an**gekommen.*	We have arrived at seven o'clock.
*Wir waren um 7 Uhr **an**gekommen.*	We had arrived at seven o'clock.
*Wir werden um 7 Uhr **an**kommen.*	We will arrive at seven o'clock.
*Wir werden um 7 Uhr **an**gekommen sein.*	We will have arrived at seven o'clock.

Whether the verb is regular or irregular and whether it takes **haben** or **sein** as its auxiliary in the perfect tenses, the separable prefix still functions in the same way. The position of the separable prefix is identical in all the above sentences.

The infinitives **sitzen**, **stecken**, and **stehen** are verbs but can also be used as separable prefixes. Their usage as such is limited primarily to two verbs: **bleiben** and **lassen**. Consider how each of these verb prefixes is used with these two verbs: **sitzenbleiben**, **steckenbleiben**, **stehenbleiben**, **sitzenlassen**, **steckenlassen**, and **stehenlassen**. First look at some example sentences with the verb **bleiben**:

Frau Schröder, bleiben Sie bitte sitzen!	Mrs. Schroeder, remain seated, please.
Mein Wagen ist wieder in der Mitte der Straße steckengeblieben.	My car got stuck in the middle of the street again.
Kinder, warum bleibt ihr noch stehen?	Children, why are you still standing?

Now consider some examples with the verb **lassen**:

Der Arzt lässt Herrn Grundig sitzen.	The doctor has Mr. Grundig sit down.
Ich habe den Schlüssel wieder steckengelassen.	I left the key in the door again.
Die Tochter hat ihre Suppe schon wieder stehengelassen.	The daughter has left her soup untouched again.

You will find a list of commonly used separable prefixes in the Quick-Glance Tables following Chapter 16.

Exercise 1

The sentences below are incomplete because they are missing the verb. Use the infinitive in parentheses and place it and its prefix in the appropriate position in two sentences. Write the verb in the present tense in the first sentence and in the present perfect tense in the second sentence. For example:

(zumachen) Er die Tür.
Er macht die Tür zu.
Er hat die Tür zugemacht.

1. (aufhören) Heute der Unterricht um 14 Uhr.

_____.

_____.

2. (anfangen) Das Konzert pünktlich.

_____.

_____.

3. (zuschlagen) Warum das Kind die Tür?

_____.

_____.

4. (nachgehen) Diese alte Armbanduhr oft eine Viertelstunde.

_____.

_____.

5. (umsteigen) Viele Reisende in Frankfurt.

_____.

_____.

Exercise 2

Rewrite each of the following present tense sentences in the present perfect tense and the future tense.

1. Mein Sohn steht täglich um 8 Uhr auf.

_____.

_____.

2. Karin zieht ihre neuen Handschuhe an.

_____.

_____.

3. Die Gäste treten in das Haus ein.

_____.

_____.

4. Viele Passagiere steigen am Bahnhof aus.

_____.

_____.

Exercise 3
Write original sentences with the following verbs.

1. einsteigen

_____.

2. mitkommen

_____.

3. durchlesen

_____.

4. zumachen

_____.

5. austrinken

_____.

Another Kind of Imperative

Imperatives are commands directed at the second person singular or plural (*you*). You cannot give a command in the first or third person; therefore, there is only one conjugational form to know for each of the three pronouns that mean *you* in German: ***du***, ***ihr***, and ***Sie***. Imperatives are always punctuated with an exclamation point.

To form an imperative correctly, you have to distinguish between verbs that have no vowel change in the present tense and those that do. The following examples require no vowel change in the present tense conjugation:

du	*ihr*	*Sie*	
Komme!	*Kommt!*	*Kommen Sie!*	(come)
Singe!	*Singt!*	*Singen Sie!*	(sing)
Warte!	*Wartet!*	*Warten Sie!*	(wait)

The ***du*** form of the imperative with no vowel change in the present tense is sometimes stated without the final vowel *-e*: *Komm! Sing!* However, verbs that have stems that end in *-d* or *-t* cannot omit the final *-e*: *Warte!*

When there is a vowel change in the present tense (e.g., ***ich sehe***, ***du siehst***, ***er sieht***, ***wir sehen***, ***ihr seht***, ***sie sehen***), that vowel change occurs in the ***du*** form of the imperative:

du	*ihr*	*Sie*	
Sieh!	*Seht!*	*Sehen Sie!*	(see)
Gib!	*Gebt!*	*Geben Sie!*	(give)
Sprich!	*Sprecht!*	*Sprechen Sie!*	(speak)

Note that the final vowel *-e* is dropped in the *du* form.

When the present tense requires an **umlaut** in the conjugation (e.g., *ich laufe*, *du läufst*, *er läuft*, *wir laufen*, *ihr lauft*, *sie laufen*), the *du* form imperative is not affected:

du	ihr	Sie	
Laufe!	Lauft!	Laufen Sie!	(run)
Fahre!	Fahrt!	Fahren Sie!	(drive)

The verb *sein* is the only verb that does not form the imperative of *du* and *Sie* from the present tense conjugation:

du	ihr	Sie	
Sei!	Seid!	Seien Sie!	(be)

Inseparable prefixes remain static in the imperative. However, separable prefixes appear at the end of an imperative sentence:

du	ihr	Sie	
Besuche!	Besucht!	Besuchen Sie!	(visit)
Erwarte!	Erwartet!	Erwarten Sie!	(expect)
Komme mit!	Kommt mit!	Kommen Sie mit!	(come along)
Gib aus!	Gebt aus!	Geben Sie aus!	(spend)

There is another form of imperative that is used without a specific second person singular or plural in mind. It occurs when someone is addressing a large group of people; it is used on signs; and it is what a person of authority says without having to direct a command to a particular person. The formation of this kind of imperative is quite simple. It is formed with an infinitive and is punctuated with an exclamation point. Here are some examples of this form of imperative:

What the stationmaster says to the people on the platform as the train is pulling in:

Zurückbleiben!   Stand back.

What the teacher says to the class:

    Aufstehen bitte!   Stand up, please.

What the warden tells the guards to do with a new prisoner:

    Abführen!   Take him away.

A sign on a wall:

    Bitte von rechts anstellen!   Please form a line on the right.

A sign in a museum:

    Nicht anfassen!   Do not touch.

A sign on the door handle of a hotel room:

    Bitte nicht stören!   Do not disturb.

Instructions at a website:

    Bitte hier klicken!   Click here, please.
    Download manuell starten!   Start the download manually.

This infinitive usage as an imperative is rare in friendly conversations because it can sound quite abrupt. It is used primarily in situations where there is no polite relationship between persons. Students of German must, of course, be aware of it, but it is used primarily by officials addressing a group or on signs.

The Imperative Expressed by the Passive Voice

The passive voice is a conjugation of the verb **werden** plus a past participle: **Es wird gemacht.** *It is being done.* **Sie wurde entlassen.** *She was let go.* But certain statements expressed in the passive voice can issue a form of command. The statements usually begin with the pronoun **es** as in the following examples:

Es wird hier nicht getanzt!	There is no dancing allowed here.
Es wird jetzt geschlafen!	It's time to get to sleep.
Es wird jetzt nicht gelacht!	There'll be no more laughing now.

This kind of imperative is quite casual and found mostly in the spoken language. Commands given in this way are rather strong and can come across as impolite.

Involving Yourself in a Command

Most imperatives or commands are directed at the second person (*du*, *ihr*, *Sie*). But just like English, German has command forms that include the person who is giving the command. In English an imperative phrase can begin with *let's*, and this suggests that the speaker intends to include himself or herself in the action of the verb. Compare the following sentences. The first three are commands given to the second person:

Go home.
Have something to drink.
Speak only German.

The next three sentences are commands that include the speaker:

Let's go home.
Let's have something to drink.
Let's speak only German.

In order to form the German imperative that includes the person giving the command, conjugate the verb in the present tense for the first person plural pronoun *wir*. Then invert the subject and verb, and you have an imperative that means *let's do something*: **Wir gehen.—Gehen wir!** *Let's go.* **Wir fangen an.—Fangen wir an!** *Let's begin.* Look at these example sentences that compare a *du* **imperative** with an imperative meaning *let's*:

Sprich nur Deutsch!	Speak only German.
Sprechen wir nur Deutsch!	Let's speak only German.

Schreibe einen Brief!	Write a letter.
Schreiben wir einen Brief!	Let's write a letter.

Now look at some example sentences that compare an ***ihr* imperative** with an imperative meaning *let's*:

Geht ins Kino!	Go to the movies.
Gehen wir ins Kino!	Let's go to the movies.
Esst zuerst!	Eat first.
Essen wir zuerst!	Let's eat first.

Now look at some example sentences that compare a ***Sie* imperative** with an imperative meaning *let's*:

Fahren Sie nach Berlin!	Drive to Berlin.
Fahren wir nach Berlin!	Let's drive to Berlin.
Trinken Sie ein Glas Bier!	Drink a glass of beer.
Trinken wir ein Glas Bier!	Let's drink a glass of beer.

Imperatives formed to address others have three forms: one for ***du,*** one for ***ihr***, and one for ***Sie***. When a command is given that includes the person giving the command, there is no distinction between formal or informal or between singular and plural.

A similar expression that can include the person who is giving the command is formed with the verb ***lassen***. But the verb ***lassen*** can also become an imperative for all three second person pronouns (***du***, ***ihr***, ***Sie***):

du	*Lass!*
ihr	*Lasst!*
Sie	*Lassen Sie!*

If you include the accusative pronoun ***uns*** with the verb ***lassen***, you have the phrase that means *let's*. And remember that you have to choose the form of imperative of ***lassen*** based upon the second person pronoun involved:

Lass uns darüber sprechen!	Let's talk about it. (speaker and one other person)
Lasst uns jetzt gehen!	Let's go now. (speaker and two or more persons)

You can use other accusative pronouns or nouns with **lassen** and still form an imperative. However, the meaning is now *let* and not *let's*:

Lass ihn nach Hause gehen!	Let him go home.
Lasst die Kinder ihnen helfen!	Let the children help them.
Lassen Sie mich bitte mitkommen!	Let me come along, please.

Exercise 1

The **du** form of the imperative is given for each phrase. Provide the **ihr** form, the **Sie** form, and the form an official would use when addressing a group.

1. Bleibe ruhig!

   _____.

   _____.

   _____.

2. Bitte steige aus!

   _____.

   _____.

   _____.

3. Lache nicht!

   _____.

   _____.

   _____.

Exercise 2

Change the following imperatives to the meaning *let's*. For example:

Geh nach Hause!
Gehen wir nach Hause!

1. Essen Sie in einem guten Restaurant!

_____.

2. Singt Weihnachtslieder!

_____.

3. Repariere Omas Wagen!

_____.

4. Reist mit dem Bus in die Schweiz!

_____.

5. Laufen Sie an die Ecke!

_____.

Exercise 3

Change the following imperatives from the infinitive type that is often used by a person of authority to address a group to a polite imperative with the pronoun *Sie*.

1. Zurückbleiben!

_____.

2. Hier aussteigen!

_____.

3. Gepäck aufmachen!

_____.

4. Nicht öffnen!

_____.

Haben or *sein*

Centuries ago, there was a time when English used two auxiliaries in the present and past perfect tenses: *have* and *be*. Transitive verbs required *have* as their auxiliary, and verbs that showed motion from one place to another used *be*. Some older forms of the Bible still show this usage of *be* as an auxiliary in phrases such as "The Lord is come." In modern English, you would say, "The Lord has come."

German and several other European languages still differentiate between transitive verbs and intransitive verbs of motion by the kind of auxiliary used in the present perfect and the past perfect tenses. But certain German verbs that do not fit neatly into these two categories also require a specific auxiliary. So how do you know which auxiliary to use? Should it be **haben**? Or should it be **sein**?

The simplest rule for determining whether a verb uses **haben** or **sein** in the perfect tenses is: **use *haben* with transitive verbs and use *sein* with intransitive verbs of motion**. Compare the pairs of phrases that follow, with transitive verbs on the left and intransitive verbs of motion on the right:

ich habe gefunden	I have found	*ich bin gegangen*	I have gone
ich hatte gefunden	I had found	*ich war gegangen*	I had gone
er hat gemacht	he has made	*er ist gefahren*	he has driven
er hatte gemacht	he had made	*er war gefahren*	he had driven

The key to identifying a transitive verb is the direct object. If there is a direct object (accusative case) in the sentence, the auxiliary will be **haben**.

*Sie haben **ihre Bücher** verloren.*	They have lost their books.
*Du hast **ihn** beleidigt.*	You have insulted him.
***Wen** haben Sie beobachtet?*	Whom have you observed?

But don't forget the dative verbs. The translation of a sentence with a dative verb into English often produces an English sentence with a direct object. But the German sentence has a dative object in it.

*Sie haben **dem Mann** geholfen.*	They have helped the man.
*Sie hat **uns** gedient.*	She has served us.
***Wem** hast du gedankt?*	Whom have you thanked?

In the case of dative verbs, the direct object can no longer be the indicator that the perfect tenses will use **haben** as their auxiliary. In fact, some dative verbs will use **haben** as their auxiliary in the perfect tenses, and others will use **sein**.

To distinguish between dative verbs that use **haben** and those that use **sein**, you have to rely on the meaning of the verb to help you choose the correct auxiliary. In general, you can use **haben** as the auxiliary of a dative verb in all cases except when the verb is a **verb of motion**. Then use **sein**. Look at these examples of dative verbs that require **haben** as their auxiliary:

*Wir **haben** vielen Touristen gedient.*	We have served many tourists.
*Frau Keller **hat** dem jungen Professor geantwortet.*	Ms. Keller has answered the young professor.
*Der Polizist **hatte** mir nicht geglaubt.*	The police officer hadn't believed me.

Now compare them to the following dative verbs of motion:

*Ich **bin** ihnen bis in die Stadt gefolgt.*	I followed them into the city.
*Der böse Hund **ist** der armen Frau entlaufen.*	The bad dog has run away from the poor woman.
*Es **war** ihr plötzlich eingefallen, dass ihm nicht zu trauen war.*	It suddenly had occurred to her that he wasn't to be trusted.

A notable exception to this rule concerning dative verbs is the verb **begegnen**. By meaning, it is not a verb of motion, but it nonetheless uses **sein** as its auxiliary.

*Ich **bin** meinem Professor in der Stadt begegnet.*	I have encountered my professor in the city.
*Da **sind** wir alten Freunden begegnet.*	We encountered old friends there.

Of course, all verbs of motion—even those that are not dative verbs of motion—use **sein** as their auxiliary in the perfect tenses. Consider these examples of **non-dative** verbs of motion:

*Um wieviel Uhr **bist** du nach Hause gekommen?*	What time did you come home?
*Johann **ist** schon aufs Land zurückgegangen.*	Johann has already gone back to the country.
*Ein junger Mann **war** über die Straße gelaufen.*	A young man had run across the street.

There is another, more graphic, way to determine whether a verb requires **haben** or **sein** in the perfect tenses: Pretend that your feet are glued to the floor. Give yourself a command to carry out the action of a verb. If it is something that you can probably do without moving your feet, the verb is transitive. It will take **haben**. If you have to move your feet to a new place to carry out the action of the verb, the verb is a verb of motion and takes **sein**.

Consider whether you would need to move your feet to perform the verbs in the examples that follow. The first three examples require no movement to carry out the action. These verbs use **haben** as their auxiliary:

*Ich **habe** ein Buch gelesen.*	I have read a book.
*Wir **haben** mit ihm gesprochen.*	We have spoken with him.
*Wer **hat** dieses Hemd gekauft?*	Who has bought this shirt?

The next three examples require movement to perform the action of the verb and use **sein** as their auxiliary:

*Hans **ist** nach Hause gelaufen.*	Hans has run home.
*Der Vogel **ist** aus dem Fenster geflogen.*	The bird has flown out the window.
***Sind** sie zum Park gegangen?*	Have they gone to the park?

Naturally, this kind of rule can only be applied in general. There are exceptions. For instance, the verb *kick* requires the movement of a foot to carry out the action. But this verb is transitive and takes a direct object. It uses **haben** as its auxiliary in the perfect tenses.

*Ich **habe** ihn mit dem Fuß gestossen.*	I kicked him with my foot.

There is another group of verbs that use **sein** as their auxiliary in the perfect tenses, but they are not verbs that show a movement from one place to another. Instead, these verbs show **states of being** or **states and conditions** that change and are out of the control of the subject.

bleiben (to stay)	This result occurs with the passage of time.
einschlafen (to fall asleep)	This happens to you unconsciously.
geschehen (to happen)	This state occurs without your direct influence over it.
passieren (to happen)	This state occurs without your direct influence over it.
sein (to be)	You exist. You have no direct control over this state.
sterben (to die)	You die. You have no direct control over this state.
werden (to become)	This state occurs without your direct influence over it.

Consider these examples of conditions over which a person has no control:

*Ich **bin** endlich um Mitternacht eingeschlafen.*	I finally fell asleep at midnight.

*Wann **ist** es geschehen?*   When did it happen?
*Der alte Graf **ist** gestorben.*   The old count has died.

Although it is logical that you do not have direct control over life, the verb **leben** is transitive and uses **haben** as its auxiliary. You can assume that **life** (***das Leben***) is the direct object of the verb.

*Ich **habe** (mein Leben) gelebt.*   I lived (my life).
*Wir **haben** (unser Leben) in*   We lived (our life) in Germany.
Deutschland gelebt.

When you add a modal auxiliary to a sentence that has a verb that requires **sein** as its auxiliary, it does not mean **sein** will be the auxiliary in the sentence. Sentences that have modal auxiliaries in them require you to conjugate the modal and not the other verb in the sentence. The other verb will be an infinitive. For example, the verbs **laufen** and **gehen** are verbs of motion and require **sein** as their auxiliary. If a modal is used with either verb in a sentence, the auxiliary will change to **haben**, as in the following examples:

*Die kleinen Kinder **sind** nicht*   The little children did not run
über die Straße gelaufen.   across the street.
*Die kleinen Kinder **haben** nicht*   The little children were not
*über die Straße laufen **dürfen**.*   allowed to run across the
                                         street.

*Die junge Dame **ist** in den Garten* The young lady went into the
gegangen.   garden.
*Die junge Dame **hat** in den*   The young lady wanted to go
*Garten gehen **wollen**.*   into the garden.

Since all modals use **haben** as their auxiliary, there are no choices to be made regarding the auxiliary when the conjugated verb is a modal. Always use **haben**.

Refer to the Quick-Glance Tables at the back of this book for a list of verbs with their appropriate auxiliary and the function of the verb (transitive, intransitive, verb of motion, verb of radical change, or dative verb).

Exercise 1

In the blank provided, fill in the appropriate form of **haben** or **sein**.

1. Ich _____ dem Professor eine interessante Frage

   gestellt.

2. Vor wieviel Jahren _____ dein Urgroßvater gestorben?

3. Das junge Pferd _____ wieder auf die Wiese gelaufen.

4. Warum _____ du so hartnäckig geworden?

5. Gudrun _____ die neue Kunsthalle besuchen wollen.

Exercise 2

Write a sentence in the present perfect tense with the verb provided in parentheses.

1. (verkaufen)

   _____.

2. (werden)

   _____.

3. (austrinken)

   _____.

4. (stehenbleiben)

   _____.

5. (danken)

   _____.

Exercise 3

Rewrite the following present tense sentences in the past, present perfect, and future tenses.

1. Ich stehe immer um halb sieben auf.

   _____ .

   _____ .

   _____ .

2. Wer versteht dieses Problem?

   _____ .

   _____ .

   _____ .

3. Willst du in die Stadt fahren?

   _____ .

   _____ .

   _____ .

Verbs Used as Other Parts of Speech

It is common in many languages that a certain part of speech (verb, noun, conjunction, etc.) is used in other ways. In English, for example, the word *book* can be used as a noun, a verb, or an adjective.

Noun: My favorite **book** is Mann's *Der Tod in Venedig*.
Verb: The thief was taken to the police station and **booked**.
Adjective: Her **book** review was very negative.

Verbs That Become Nouns

Sometimes the form of a word is changed slightly when it becomes a new part of speech. In English, a verb attaches the ending **-ing**, and then it can be used as a noun.

to cry   She uses **crying** as a weapon.
to write   **Writing** is my favorite pastime.

An infinitive can also be used as a noun.

to err   **To err** is human.
to swim   My goal is **to swim** the length of the pool.

German does something similar. It uses verbs as nouns, and it uses infinitives as nouns just like English. When a German infinitive becomes a noun, it can only be used as a singular—there is no plural form—and the gender is always neuter.

das Arbeiten	to work, working
das Einkommen	income (financial)
das Leben	life

Since such infinitives are used as nouns, it means that they can be declined just like other nouns. And since they are neuter nouns, they follow the declensional pattern of all other neuter nouns. Compare the declension of the neuter noun **das Haus** with the infinitive used as a noun **das Essen**:

nominative case	*das Haus*	*das Essen*
accusative case	*das Haus*	*das Essen*
dative case	*dem Haus*	*dem Essen*
genitive case	*des Hauses*	*des Essens*

Sometimes infinitive-nouns are used in special or pat expressions. Often there is a corresponding English expression, which must be used in the translation of the German expression. **Rennen**, for example, means *to run* or *to race*. It is also the noun for *a run* or *a race*. But its meaning is altered slightly when it appears in special phrases like the following:

Die Läufer erreichen das Ziel	The runners reach the finish at
gleichzeitig. Es ist ein totes	the same time. It's a dead heat.
Rennen.	

It is important to be cautious when using infinitives as nouns. Always be aware of any nuance of meaning that might occur in special phrases or in certain pat expressions.

Sometimes verbs become nouns by making a slight change in the form of the word. In English, it is common to change vowels or consonants in a verb from one of its principal parts in order to form a noun, as in the formation of the noun *gift*:

give, gave, given   gift

In German many nouns are also formed from one of the principal parts of a verb and sometimes with a slight change of the verb's vowels or consonants. Often, nouns formed in this way end in *-e*, and they are **usually** feminine in gender.

gibt, gab, gegeben	*die Gabe*	gift, talent
hilft, half, geholfen	*die Hilfe*	help, aid

When a noun is formed in this way from a verb that has multiple prefixes, those prefixes remain attached to the noun formation.

abnehmen	*die Abnahme*	decline
ausnehmen	*die Ausnahme*	exception
zunehmen	*die Zunahme*	increase

Another high-frequency noun that is formed in this way comes from the verb *glauben*. However, the gender of the noun is masculine although the noun in the nominative case can end in *-e* and, thus, have the appearance of a feminine noun. The ending of this noun in the nominative case can also be *-en*.

glauben	*der Glaube, Glauben*	belief

Compare the declension of *der Glaube(n)* with a feminine noun formed from the verb *reisen*:

	glauben	*reisen*
nominative case	*der Glaube(n)*	*die Reise*
accusative case	*den Glauben*	*die Reise*
dative case	*dem Glauben*	*der Reise*
genitive case	*des Glaubens*	*der Reise*

A large number of nouns are formed from verbs by adding the suffix *-ung* to the verb. Nouns formed in this way are always feminine in gender.

abrüsten	*die Abrüstung*	disarmament
bedeuten	*die Bedeutung*	meaning

When a verb has multiple prefixes, those prefixes remain attached to the verb when it becomes a noun with the suffix *-ung*.

anstellen	*die Anstellung*	employment
ausstellen	*die Ausstellung*	exhibition
vorstellen	*die Vorstellung*	imagination

There are numerous other ways that nouns are formed from verbs or from one of their principal parts. Following are examples of some of the most commonly encountered forms:

Nouns formed with the suffix *-NIS*

bekennen	*das Bekenntnis*	acknowledgment
verstehen	*das Verständnis*	comprehension

Nouns related to the verb *LAUFEN*

ablaufen	*der Ablauf*	running off
auslaufen	*der Auslauf*	leakage

Nouns related to the verb *GEHEN*

ausgehen	*der Ausgang*	exit
eingehen	*der Eingang*	entrance

Nouns related to the verb *KOMMEN*

ankommen	*die Ankunft*	arrival
unterkommen	*die Unterkunft*	shelter

Nouns related to the verb *SEHEN*

absehen	*die Absicht*	intention
ansehen	*die Ansicht*	view

Notice that the relationship of the noun to the verb is not always clear. In the case of **Ablauf**, the link to **laufen** is evident. Even with **Ausgang**, you can see the relationship to the principal parts of **gehen** (**geht**, **ging**, **gegangen**). But the relationship is more obscure with **Ankunft** and **kommen** and with **Absicht** and **sehen**.

These are not the only verbs that form nouns in this manner. There are many others. But by examining these, you can grasp how verbs become nouns and develop an intuition about their meaning.

There is another very large category of nouns that are formed from verbs, and they look, at first glance, like past participles. They have the appearance of past participles because they begin with the prefix *ge-*. But these are nouns derived from verbs or from one of their principal parts as in the following examples:

brauchen	*der Gebrauch*	use
flüstern	*das Geflüster*	whispering
hören	*das Gehör*	hearing

Do be aware that many nouns that begin with the prefix **ge-** are **not** formed from a verb, for example, **Getreide**, **Gemüse**, and **Gemeinde**.

Verbs That Become Adjectives and Adverbs

Many adjectives and adverbs are derived from verbs. In English this is as common as it is in German. Sometimes native speakers do not even realize that the adjective or adverb they are using is the offspring of a verb. In English this obscurity of the verbal origin of a modifier occurs most often when the spelling of the adjectival or adverbial form is somewhat different from that of the verb itself, as for example in *to eat—edible*. But in other cases, the root and the new forms are obviously related.

care	careful	carefully
hope	hopeless	hopelessly

Such adjectival and adverbial derivations from verbs also occur in German. Sometimes the adjectives and adverbs make a detour through a noun on the way to the new form, but in general you can say that many hundreds of adjectives and adverbs come from verbs. Being aware of this relationship is an important tool for the student of German. It means not having to look up every word encountered if you are able to identify the verb that the modifier comes from.

There are certain prominent suffixes that become attached to a verb to make it a modifier. Some of the suffixes give a specially flavored meaning to the new modifier, although in most cases the original meaning of the verb is still—at least partly—intact.

A high-frequency suffix is *-sam*. Look at the following examples of verbs that become modifiers and their English translations:

bedeuten	*bedeutsam*	significant
gehorchen	*gehorsam*	obedient
sparen	*sparsam*	thrifty, economical

Another common suffix is *-lich*. But this suffix does not give a clear meaning to the new modifier derived, nor is it always used directly on the verb stem itself. In some cases this suffix is applied to the noun that comes from the verb. Consider these examples of verbs that become modifiers (sometimes by means of their noun form):

absehen	*Absicht*	*absichtlich*	intentional
eindringen		*eindringlich*	penetrating
verstehen	*Verstand*	*verständlich*	understandable

Yet another suffix that serves to make a verb into an adjective or adverb is *-ig*. A few of the examples that follow are formed from the noun that is derived from the verb:

bluten	*Blut*	*blutig*	bloody
sorgen	*Sorgfalt*	*sorgfältig*	careful
trauen	*Trauer*	*traurig*	sad

The suffix *-bar* is very commonly used and often implies ability in some activity.

beweisen	*beweisbar*	provable
brechen	*brechbar*	breakable
lesen	*lesbar*	legible

The suffix *-los* can be equated with the English suffix *-less*. It is found attached to the stem of German verbs and is easily translated into English. In a few instances, it makes its journey to becoming a modifier by way of the verb's noun form.

besinnen	*Sinn*	*sinnlos*	senseless, thoughtless
sorgen	*Sorge*	*sorglos*	carefree, careless
sprechen	*Sprache*	*sprachlos*	speechless

Another very common suffix is **-isch**, which indicates that someone or something has the quality of the meaning of the verb from which it is derived.

kämpfen	*Kämpfer*	*kämpferisch*	warlike
murren		*mürrisch*	morose, surly
stürmen		*stürmisch*	stormy

When using **-fähig** as a suffix, you are saying that someone or something is capable of performing in a certain way.

lehren	*lehrfähig*	capable of being taught, teachable
tragen	*tragfähig*	capable of carrying a load or heavy weight
urteilen	*urteilsfähig*	capable of judging, judicious

The suffix **-würdig** is used to mean *worthy* or *deserving* and follows the stem or infinitive of a small number of verbs.

lieben	*liebenswürdig*	kind, amiable
merken	*merkwürdig*	noteworthy, remarkable
sehen	*sehenswürdig*	worth seeing

The suffix **-weise** is comparable to the English suffix *-wise*, as in the modifier *clockwise* (**uhrweise**). It can be used as a suffix for nouns such as **Uhr** and nouns derived from a verb.

wechseln	*Wechsel*	*wechselweise*	mutually, reciprocally

These are only a small sampling of the kinds of suffixes that change verbs into modifiers. Many others exist, which you will encounter on your journey through the German language.

Note that all these modifiers shown as adjectives have their adverbial usage as well. For example, **absichtlich** means *intentional* or *intentionally* depending on its function in the sentence.

Whether adjective or adverb, these modifiers can be used like any other modifier in a German sentence. When they are used as adjectives, you must provide for **gender**, **number**, and **case**. Here are a few examples:

*Diese Balken sind alt und schwach und nicht mehr **tragfähig**.*	These beams are old and weak and no longer capable of bearing a load.
*Ein **brechbares** Spielzeug ist für kein Kind geeignet.*	A breakable toy isn't suitable for any child.
*Der Lehrer ist nur den **gehorsamen** Schülern gegenüber freundlich.*	The teacher is only kind to the obedient pupils.

With knowledge about how modifiers are formed, you can, with experience, learn to create your own adjectives and adverbs that fit the meaning of what you wish to say or write. At the same time, you will be more disposed to quickly grasp the intended meaning when you encounter modifiers that are derived from verbs. This is also true of nouns formed from verbs. But experience and practice are essential.

Exercise 1

Fill in the blank with the noun form of the given verb. Also include the direct article with the correct gender. For example:

helfen die Hilfe (help)

1. riechen _____ (*odor*)

2. glauben _____ (*belief*)

3. singen _____ (*singing*)

4. bedeuten _____ (*meaning*)

5. arbeiten _____ (*work*)

6. leben _____ (*life*)

7. malen _____ (*painting*)

8. wohnen _____ (*apartment*)

9. abrüsten _____ (*disarmament*)

10. vorsehen _____ (*caution*)

Exercise 2

Fill in the blank with the infinitive from which the noun provided was derived. For example:

die Hilfe (help) <u>*helfen*</u>

1. der Gebrauch (*use*) _____

2. das Einkommen (*income*) _____

3. die Erzählung (*story*) _____

4. die Kenntnis (*knowledge*) _____

5. der Eingang (*entrance*) _____

6. die Absicht (*intention*) _____

7. das Schauspiel (*play*) _____

8. der Gelehrte (*scholar*) _____

9. das Lernen (*learning*) _____

10. das Soll und Haben (*debit and credit*) _____

Exercise 3

Fill in the blank with the infinitive from which the modifier provided was derived. For example:

gehorsam (obedient) <u>gehorchen</u>

1. absichtlich (*intentional*) _____

2. klangreich (*sonorous*) _____

3. lehrfähig (*capable of being taught*) _____

4. kämpferisch (*warlike*) _____

5. blutig (*bloody*) _____

6. beweisbar (*provable*) _____

7. verdächtig (*suspicious*) _____

8. anspruchsvoll (*pretentious*) _____

9. wechselweise (*mutually, reciprocally*) _____

10. merkwürdig (*noteworthy*) _____

Infinitives Used with *zu*

The use of **zu** with German infinitives should not be confused with the translation of infinitives into English as *to go*, *to run*, *to play*, and so on. That use of *to* is a part of the total English infinitive. There are times, however, when the particle word *to* can be omitted in English:

I should **go**.
Must you **run** so fast?
They will **play** in the backyard.

With certain auxiliaries English can leave out the particle word *to*. This does not change the use of the German infinitive. Whether or not there is the particle word *to* in the English infinitive, the German infinitive remains constant. In the following examples, the English infinitive does not require the particle word *to*:

*Ich soll **gehen**.*	I should go.
*Musst du so schnell **laufen**?*	Must you run so fast?
*Sie werden im Garten **spielen**.*	They will play in the backyard.

In the sentences that follow, the particle word *to* is used with the infinitives:

*Ich will **mitgehen**.*	I want **to** go along.
*Ich kann schneller **laufen**.*	I am able **to** run faster.
*Er will Schach **spielen**.*	He wants **to** play chess.

Despite the differences in the two sets of English examples above, the German sentences remained constant, using simply infinitives ending in **-en**.

But there are numerous other instances where German requires the word *zu* to precede an infinitive. These phrases are infinitive phrases or clauses. For example, after the pronouns *etwas* and *nichts* it is common to use such an infinitive phrase.

Haben Sie wirklich etwas zu sagen?	Do you really have something to say?
Es gibt nichts zu essen.	There's nothing to eat.

When an adjective is used as a noun after *etwas* or *nichts*, a similar infinitive phrase is still possible.

Ich brauche etwas Interessantes zu lesen.	I need something interesting to read.
Der Reporter hat nichts Neues zu berichten.	The reporter has nothing new to report.

The same kind of infinitive phrase is found in certain idioms, as in these examples:

Ich habe mit dir ein Hühnchen zu rupfen.	I've got a bone to pick with you.
Er scheint dir Augen zu machen.	He seems to be making eyes at you.

In Chapter 2 you discovered that certain verbs, along with the modal auxiliaries, require a double infinitive structure in the perfect and future tenses. These verbs are *helfen*, *hören*, *lassen*, *sehen*, *gehen*, and *lernen*. Following is a reminder of how these verbs appear in the present perfect, the future, and the past tense:

Martin hat seine Schwester singen hören.	Martin heard his sister singing.
Wirst du deinen Wagen reparieren lassen?	Are you going to have your car repaired?
Ich sah die Lehrlinge arbeiten.	I saw the apprentices working.
Sie geht morgen segeln.	She's going sailing tomorrow.

Note that the infinitives in sentences with the verbs **hören**, **lassen**, **sehen**, and **gehen** do not require **zu**. In the case of **helfen** and **lernen**, however, the general rules that govern modal auxiliaries and **helfen**, **hören**, **lassen**, **sehen**, **gehen**, and **lernen** regarding infinitive usage sometimes cease to apply. If the infinitive clause is long, there is a tendency to use **zu** with an infinitive following either **helfen** or **lernen**.

Ich half dem Chef einen wichtigen Bericht über das neue Produkt **zu** *schreiben.*	I helped the boss write an important report about the new product.
Sie lernte ihren eigenen Computer **zu** *programmieren.*	She learned to program her own computer.

It is important to remember that this use of **zu** does not occur with the modal auxiliaries or the verbs **hören**, **lassen**, **sehen**, and **gehen**.

As you have learned, prefixes have a specific function with verbs. Some are inseparable and others are separable, and each type reacts slightly differently in infinitive clauses. If the verb in the infinitive clause has an inseparable prefix (**be-**, **emp-**, **ent-**, **er-**, **ge-**, **ver-**, **zer-**), the prefix remains on the stem of the verb and **zu** precedes the verb. The infinitive phrase is written as two words: **zu** and the infinitive.

Der kleine Junge verspricht sich besser **zu** *benehmen.*	The little boy promises to behave himself better.
Der schläfrige Student versucht alles **zu** *verstehen.*	The sleepy student is trying to understand everything.
Die Soldaten haben vor das ganze Dorf **zu** *zerstören.*	The soldiers intend to destroy the whole village.

The separable prefixes, however, react differently. Some of the most frequently used of the separable prefixes are **ab-**, **an-**, **aus-**, **bei-**, **her-**, **hin-**, **mit-**, **nach-**, **vor-**, and **zu-**. You will find a list of separable prefixes in the Quick-Glance Tables following Chapter 16.

A separable prefix on a verb that is in an infinitive clause will separate from the stem of the verb by the addition of **zu**. The new infinitive is written as one word.

*Angelika hatte vor ins Kino
mit**zu**kommen.*

Angelika intended to come along
to the movies.

*Es war ihm schwer seine Gefühle
aus**zu**drücken.*

It was hard for him to express his
feelings.

*Mutter versucht ihm das Gedicht
bei**zu**bringen.*

Mother tries to teach him the
poem.

Infinitives are often used with modal auxiliaries. The modal is the conjugated verb, and the infinitive is the last element in the sentence or clause.

Willst du aufs Land fahren?

Do you want to drive into the
country?

Martin konnte nichts verstehen.

Martin couldn't understand
anything.

These two elements—a modal and an infinitive—can also be used together with **zu** to form an infinitive phrase or clause. The word **zu** must stand between the infinitive and the modal auxiliary in this kind of structure, and the modal auxiliary, preceded by **zu**, is the last element in the infinitive phrase.

*Ich war empört wieder zu Hause
bleiben **zu** müssen.*

I was upset to have to stay at
home again.

*Klaudia ist dankbar den jungen
Rockstar kennenlernen **zu** dürfen.*

Klaudia is grateful to be allowed
to meet the young rock star.

The future tense is composed of a conjugation of **werden** plus an infinitive.

*Ich werde ihm einen Brief
schreiben.*

I'll write him a letter.

Was wird passieren?

What's going to happen?

The future perfect tense is similar to the future tense but does not end with an infinitive alone. Instead the final component of this tense is a participle followed by either **haben** or **sein**, depending upon the kind of verb the participle comes from.

Sie werden bald entschieden haben.   They will soon have decided.
Er wird bis elf Uhr   He will have returned by eleven
  zurückgekommen sein.   o'clock.

Participles followed by **haben** or **sein** (e.g., **entschieden haben**, **zurückgekommen sein**) can also be used in infinitive phrases or clauses with **zu**. Notice that the word **zu** stands between the participle and the auxiliary **haben** or **sein**:

Der Wissenschaftler glaubt eine   The scientist believes to have
  *Lösung gefunden **zu** haben.*   found a solution.
Sie behauptete dem Kanzler   She claimed to have encountered
  *begegnet **zu** sein.*   the chancellor.

The passive voice consists of a conjugation of **werden** and a past participle of a transitive verb.

Die Scheune wurde zerstört.   The barn was destroyed.
Sie wird von einer Freundin   She is being called by a friend.
  angerufen.

A passive infinitive can be formed by combining a past participle of a transitive verb with the infinitive **werden**: **zerstört werden**, **angerufen werden**, **gefunden werden**, etc. That structure can be used in the formation of an infinitive phrase or clause with **zu**. Once again the participle and the infinitive **werden** are separated by the word **zu**.

Ich freue mich als Mitglied   I'm happy to be accepted as a
  *aufgenommen **zu** werden.*   member.
Ihm hat es gefallen von den   He liked being admired by the
  *Mädchen bewundert **zu** werden.*   girls.

In English there are many sentences that use the pronoun *it* as their subject and introduce or anticipate what will be stated in the infinitive clause of the same sentence. The idea that is introduced or anticipated by *it* can be identified by asking *what* in place of *it*.

It is impossible to work this out. (What is impossible? "to work this out")

It was rare to find fossils in this region. (What was rare? "to find fossils in this region")

This kind of structure exists in German, too. The pronoun *es* is used to introduce or anticipate an idea that occurs in the infinitive phrase or clause.

Es war nicht wichtig darüber zu berichten.	It wasn't important to report about that.
Es scheint ein Problem gewesen zu sein.	It seems to have been a problem.
Es freut mich Ihre Eltern kennenzulernen.	I'm happy to meet your parents.
Es ist schade von einem Freund betrogen zu werden.	It's a pity to be deceived by a friend.

Notice in the examples above that each sentence contains a different kind of infinitive structure: *zu berichten*—a simple infinitive phrase; *gewesen zu sein*—a past participle with an auxiliary in infinitive form; *kennenzulernen*—a prefix separated from the infinitive by *zu*; and *betrogen zu werden*—a passive infinitive.

Prepositional adverbs are phrases that form to replace a preposition and an inanimate pronoun. Pronouns replace animate nouns in prepositional phrases, and prepositional adverbs replace inanimate pronouns in prepositional phrases.

bei der Frau	*bei ihr*
mit dem Mann	*mit ihm*
um die Ecke	*darum* (not *um sie*)
von dem Haus	*davon* (not *von es*)

When a prepositional adverb introduces or anticipates an infinitive, the infinitive phrase or clause must include *zu*.

*Ich habe mich **darauf** gefreut, eine Reise nach China **zu** machen.*	I looked forward to taking a trip to China.
*Sie war **daran** interessiert, Spanisch oder Italienisch **zu** lernen.*	She was interested in learning Spanish or Italian.
*Habt ihr **davon** gesprochen, den Flug nach Moskau **zu** verschieben?*	Did you talk about postponing the flight to Moscow?

Careful! Notice that the English translations of these sentences do not use an infinitive after the preposition: *to taking a trip, in learning Spanish*, and *about postponing the fight*. English tends to use a present participle.

There are a couple pat phrases that are commonly heard in German that use an infinitive phrase with **zu**. The tense of these sentences can change, and the subject can be altered as well, but, in general, these phrases are static.

Ich habe zu tun.	I'm busy. (I have things to do.)
Es ist nicht zu glauben.	It's unbelievable. (It's not to be believed.)

Some important infinitive clauses are formed with certain prepositions: **anstatt**, **ohne**, and **um**. The preposition introduces the infinitive clause, and **zu** followed by the infinitive ends the clause.

anstatt . . . zu	instead of (doing something)
ohne . . . zu	without (doing something)
um . . . zu	in order to (do something)

Note that the English translation of these phrases is not always an infinitive.

Each of these phrases requires an infinitive at the end of the clause, and that infinitive can be a single infinitive, a past participle with an auxiliary as an infinitive, a passive infinitive, or a modal auxiliary with an infinitive.

Martin lief ins brennende Haus, um seine Schwester zu retten.	Martin ran into the burning house in order to save his sister.

Er arbeitete bis spät abends, um seine Dissertation bis Freitag beendet zu haben.	He worked late into the night in order to have finished his dissertation by Friday.
Gudrun glaubte ihm nicht, um nicht wieder betrogen zu werden.	Gudrun didn't believe him in order not to be deceived again.
Sie musste aufstehen, um den Film sehen zu können.	She had to stand up in order to see the film.

It is often possible to use all three of these prepositional phrases with the same or similar sentences, changing only the meaning according to the meaning of the infinitive phrase itself.

Johannes fordert Geld von mir, um die Miete bezahlen zu können.	Johannes demands money from me in order to pay his rent.
Johannes fordert Geld von mir, ohne mir dafür zu danken.	Johannes demands money from me without thanking me for it.
Johannes fordert Geld von mir, anstatt Arbeit zu suchen.	Johannes demands money from me instead of looking for work.

The use of **um . . . zu, ohne . . . zu**, and **anstatt . . . zu** is very common and occurs with any variety of infinitive phrases.

Er sprang schnell über den Zaun, um von dem Hund nicht gebissen zu werden.	He quickly jumped the fence in order not to be bitten by the dog.
Er sprang schnell über den Zaun, ohne sich zu besinnen.	He quickly jumped the fence without a moment's thought about it.
Er sprang schnell über den Zaun, anstatt ins Haus zu kommen.	He quickly jumped the fence instead of coming into the house.

Exercise 1

Not all the sentences below require **zu** with the infinitive. Fill in the appropriate blanks where **zu** is needed, or leave them blank if **zu** is not needed.

1. Wir hoffen bestimmt euch bald _____ besuchen.

2. Wodurch kann man eine fremde Sprache _____ lernen?

3. Es war unmöglich dieses Problem _____ lösen.

4. Ich habe einen neuen Wagen gekauft, um eine Fahrt nach Paris _____ machen.

5. Wann wirst du meine Dissertation _____ lesen?

6. Er schweigt, anstatt die Wahrheit _____ sagen.

7. Sie freuen sich darauf, eine neue Stellung in der Stadt _____ finden.

8. Es war traurig von einem Verwandten belogen _____ werden.

9. Die Kinder werden von der Lehrerin gelobt _____ werden.

10. Sie schrie vor Angst, anstatt dem alten Mann _____ helfen.

Exercise 2

Restate the **dass** clause of each sentence as an infinitive clause with **zu**.
For example:

Er empfiehlt dem Studenten, dass er diesen Roman liest.
Er empfielt dem Studenten diesen Roman zu lesen.

1. Martin warnt seinen Freund, dass er sein Geld nicht
   verschwendet.

   _____.

2. Ich bitte Sie, dass Sie morgen mitkommen.

   _____.

3. Das heiße Wetter zwingt uns, dass wir leichtere Kleidung tragen.

   _____.

4. Frau Bauer forderte von Herrn Braun, dass er die Miete bezahlt.

   _____.

5. Ich rate euch, dass ihr langsamer esst und trinkt.

   _____.

6. Der Chef befiehlt dem neuen Lehrling, dass er besser arbeitet.

   _____.

7. Vater erlaubt den Kindern nicht, dass sie zum Tanz gehen.

   _____.

8. Benno bittet seinen Vater, dass er ein Märchen liest.

   _____.

9. Wir bitten den Professor, dass er die Geschichte übersetzt.

_____ .

10. Ich habe ihm geraten, dass er einen Rechtsanwalt befragt.

_____ .

Exercise 3
Use the phrases given below to write sentences with infinitive clauses with
zu. For example:

es freut uns
Es freut uns Sie endlich kennenzulernen.

1. um . . . zu

_____ .

2. es ist nicht möglich

_____ .

3. anstatt . . . zu

_____ .

4. er bittet mich

_____ .

5. ohne . . . zu

_____ .

Ist geboren and *wurde geboren*

The verb **gebären** is a transitive verb that means *to bear* as in *to bear a child*. Most students of German are aware of its participial form **geboren**, which is so frequently used to express when someone was born:

Ich bin am zehnten Mai geboren.   I was born on the tenth of May.

Gebären does have other tense forms, which are also used for its basic meaning *to bear a child*. The verb is irregular in all tenses:

Present Tense	Past Tense	Imperative
ich gebäre	*ich gebar*	
du gebierst	*du gebarst*	*Gebier!*
sie gebiert	*sie gebar*	
wir gebären	*wir gebaren*	
ihr gebärt	*ihr gebart*	*Gebärt!*
Sie gebären	*Sie gebaren*	*Gebären Sie!*

Perfect Tenses	Future Tenses
sie hat geboren	*sie wird gebären*
sie hatte geboren	*sie wird geboren haben*

The most frequent use of this verb is, of course, the statement that tells when someone was born. This usage puts the verb in the passive voice, which is formed with a conjugation of **werden** plus the past participle of the verb **gebären—wurde geboren**. Another passive form is a conjugation of **sein** plus the past participle of **gebären—ist geboren**. This second passive gives the past participle an adjectival meaning. The same thing occurs in English. Compare these sentences:

Das Haus wird zerstört.	The house is being destroyed.
Das Haus ist zerstört.	The house is destroyed.

The second sentence of each pair, with *sein* and **to be**, uses the participles *zerstört* and **destroyed** as adjectives.

This difference in passive forms is important with the use of the verb *gebären*. If the passive is formed with *sein*, the meaning suggests that the person in question is still alive:

*Mein Vater **ist** im Juli geboren.*	My father was born in July.
*Die Kinder **sind** in Paris geboren.*	The children were born in Paris.

But when you use the past tense of *werden* to form the passive of *gebären*, the meaning suggests that the person in question is deceased:

*Wann **wurde** Beethoven geboren?*	When was Beethoven born?
*Nero **wurde** in Rom geboren.*	Nero was born in Rome.

The same participle has a couple of other important uses. It is used where in English we would say the word *native*; in this form it is used as an adjective.

Ein geborener Deutscher.	A native German.
Eine geborene Münchnerin.	A native of Munich.

This participle can also be used to express a maiden name or the word *née* to identify a maiden name:

Ilse Schmidt, geboren Braun.	Ilse Schmidt, née Braun.
Was für eine Geborene ist sie?	What's her maiden name?

As simple as this verb may seem at first glance, it has several nuances that must be considered. Because this verb is used so often in the language, it is wise to have a full understanding of these.

Exercise 1

Fill in the blank with the missing element of the conjugation of the verb *gebären*.

1. Sind deine Eltern in Deutschland _____?

2. In welchem Jahre wurde Goethe _____?

3. Luise ist verheiratet. Sie heißt jetzt Luise Dorf, _____

    Schuhmann.

4. Bismarck _____ im 19. Jahrhundert geboren.

Exercise 2

Form sentences that tell when the person described was born.

1. George Washington/1732

    _____.

2. der Tennisspieler/Boris Becker/22.11.1967

    _____.

3. die Zwillinge/2005

    _____.

4. Wolfgang Amadeus Mozart/27.Januar 1756

    _____.

13

Present and Past Participles

Present and past participles exist in both English and German. In English, the present participle is used with a conjugation of *to be* to describe an action in progress or still incomplete. A present participle is formed from the infinitive of the verb with the ending *-ing*:

I am **learning** German and Arabic.
Were you all **singing** the same song?

Present participles can also be used as adjectives:

I love the sound of **flowing** water.
The **colliding** automobiles made a horrible sound.

Past participles are used with a conjugation of *to have* to form the perfect tenses:

She has **borrowed** my car again.
By Wednesday we shall have **traveled** over a thousand miles.

And like present participles, past participles can act as adjectives:

Who's responsible for the **broken** lamp?
The regularly **scheduled** meeting had to be cancelled.

German present and past participles function in much the same way. They are derived from verbs but have uses that go beyond what a conjugated verb has. A conjugated verb has forms that identify the tense of a sentence: *ich sehe*—present tense; *wir gingen*—past tense; *er hat gesprochen*—present perfect tense; *er wird singen*—future tense. Participles go beyond tense identification and can serve as modifiers or nouns.

Present participles are formed quite simply: the suffix **-d** is added to an infinitive. The new meaning made from the addition of this suffix is the German translation of the English infinitive plus the ending **-ing**:

entsprechen	*entsprechend*	corresponding
folgen	*folgend*	following
lesen	*lesend*	reading

When forming a present participle, there is no need to give special consideration to verbs that have separable or inseparable prefixes. Prefixes have no influence on the formation of present participles:

austrinken	*austrinkend*	finishing drinking
ertrinken	*ertrinkend*	drowning
trinken	*trinkend*	drinking

Present participles can be used as adjectives. That means that the appropriate adjective ending for gender, number, and case is added to the present participle:

die folgenden Wörter	the following words
der folgende Satz	the following sentence

Participles can also be used as nouns, and the endings required for present-participle nouns are the same as for adjectives:

die Sterbende	the dying woman
für den kranken Reisenden	for the sick traveler
mit dem Schlafenden	with the sleeping man

Past participles are formed according to the pattern for regular verbs (**gesagt**, **eingestimmt**, **verlacht**, etc.) or according to the pattern for irregular verbs (**gesehen**, **vorgekommen**, **entlaufen**, etc.). In both cases the English meaning is the translation of the past participle.

entlassen	*entlassen*	released, fired
lehren	*gelehrt*	taught, educated
verkaufen	*verkauft*	sold

Prefixes on past participles must be considered. Some of the separable prefixes are **ab-**, **an-**, **aus-**, **ein-**, **hin-**, **mit-**, **nach-**, **vor-**, and **zu-**; they are separated from the participle by the prefix **ge-**. Inseparable prefixes (**be-**, **er-**, **emp-**, **ent-**, **ge-**, **ver-**, **zer-**) do not require the prefix **ge-** in the participial formation.

austrinken	*aus**ge**trunken*	finished drinking
ertrinken	*ertrunken*	drowned
trinken	*getrunken*	drunk

Just like present participles, past participles can be used as adjectives and conform to the appropriate adjective endings:

der neulich angestellte Arbeiter	the recently employed laborer
ein bekanntes Gesicht	a familiar face

They can also be used as nouns, and the endings for past-participle nouns are the same as for adjectives:

ein Gelehrter	a scholar, educated man
gegen den Verhafteten	against the arrested man
von meinen deutschen Verwandten	from my German relatives

Compare the endings of present and past participles in all the cases with the two phrases **das schlafende Kind** and **der gemähte Rasen**:

NOMINATIVE

Das schlafende Kind lag auf dem Bett.	The sleeping child lay on the bed.
Der gemähte Rasen sieht wie ein Teppich aus.	The mown lawn looks like a carpet.

ACCUSATIVE

Vater legte das schlafende Kind auf das Sofa.	Father laid the sleeping child on the sofa.
Mein Onkel bewunderte den gemähten Rasen.	My uncle admired the mown lawn.

DATIVE

Die Puppe gehört dem schlafenden Kind.	The doll belongs to the sleeping child.
Ein Hund saß auf dem gemähten Rasen.	A dog was sitting on the mown lawn.

GENITIVE

Das Spielzeug des schlafenden Kindes war kaputt.	The sleeping child's toy was broken.
Wegen des gemähten Rasens durften wir nicht im Garten spielen.	Because of the mown lawn we couldn't play in the garden.

Take note that the endings for participles are the same as for any other adjectives, and whether a participle is a present or past participle has no influence on the declensional endings.

In some cases, participles function in an extended modifier (**erweiterte Beifügung**), which takes the elements of a relative clause and repositions them as an adjective that is modifying a noun. The whole phrase becomes the modifier. Notice that the noun can often be omitted:

RELATIVE CLAUSE

*Der Mann, **der aus dem Haus gerettet wurde**, lag auf der Straße.*	The man who was rescued from the house lay on the street.

EXTENDED MODIFIER

*Der **aus dem Haus Gerettete** lag auf der Straße.* or *Der **aus dem Haus gerettete** Mann lag auf der Straße.*	The man who was rescued from the house lay on the street.

By now you should understand the formation of present and past participles. It is important to remember that participles can function like adjectives. They must show gender, number, and case like adjectives. And like adjectives, they can act as nouns.

Exercise 1

Rewrite each verb as a present participle and as a past participle.

1. zeigen _____

2. vergehen _____

3. vergessen _____

4. annehmen _____

5. schlafen _____

6. verbrechen _____

7. einladen _____

8. schließen _____

9. bewegen _____

10. umsteigen _____

Exercise 2

Fill in the blank with the past participle of the verb form shown. Add the appropriate adjective ending.

1. (zerbrechen) Die _____ Vase lag auf dem Boden.

2. (verlieren) Sie hat den _____ Ring gefunden.

3. (senden) Ein _____ wurde nach London geschickt.

4. (ertrinken) Die Polizisten holen den _____ Mann aus dem Wasser heraus.

5. (ausbessern) Der Schuhmacher zeigte uns die _____ Schuhe.

6. (lehren) Der junge _____ schreibt eine Dissertation.

7. (verwandt) Wohnen deine _____ noch in Frankreich?

14

The Passive Voice

Passive voice verbs are altered by the tenses just like any other verb. But because of its unique structure, you need to look at the passive voice a little more closely. In English we use a conjugation of the verb *to be* followed by a **transitive** past participle. That's an important fact. Only transitive verbs—verbs that can take a direct object—can be used in passive voice sentences.

The passive voice uses elements of a sentence in the active voice to form a new kind of sentence, but one that still gives the same information as the active voice sentence. Let's look at an example:

Active voice   John kisses Mary.
Passive voice   Mary is being kissed by John.

As you can see, the subject of the active voice sentence is put in a passive position in the passive voice sentence and becomes the object of the preposition *by*. The passive voice sentence contains all the same information as the active voice sentence. It's just all stated in a new way.

The passive voice comes in handy when a speaker or writer wishes to take the blame away from the person who carries out the action of the verb. The subject of an active voice sentence can be omitted from the passive voice sentence, thus eliminating the cause or the person responsible for the action.

Active voice   The thief robbed her in broad daylight.
Passive voice   She was robbed in broad daylight.

Active voice   The mayor will call for new taxes.
Passive voice   New taxes will be called for.

In the examples above, the persons responsible for the action (the thief, the mayor) become blameless in the passive voice sentences.

German approaches the passive voice in much the same way. The basic German formation of the passive voice is a conjugation of **werden** with a transitive past participle: **wird gesucht**, **wurde gebrochen**, and so forth.

This voice is called *passive* because the subject of the active sentence becomes in the passive sentence the object of the preposition **von** and is located in a passive position in the sentence.

ACTIVE VOICE
Die Touristen *besuchten das neue Stadion.*

The tourists visited the new stadium.

PASSIVE VOICE
Das neue Stadion wurde **von den Touristen** *besucht.*

The new stadium was visited by the tourists.

Just as the cause or the person responsible for the action can be omitted in the English passive voice, so, too, can this occur in German:

ACTIVE VOICE
Herr Schmidt *hat den Manager entlassen.*

Mr. Schmidt has fired the manager.

PASSIVE VOICE
Der Manager ist entlassen worden.

The manager has been fired.

Let's look at how the German active voice sentence becomes a passive voice sentence:

ACTIVE VOICE
Der Professor fragte uns.

The professor questioned us.

PASSIVE VOICE
Wir wurden von dem Professor gefragt.

We were questioned by the professor.

The accusative direct object **uns** of the active voice sentence became the nominative subject **wir** in the passive voice sentence, and the verb was, therefore, conjugated in the plural: ***wir wurden***. The nominative subject of the active voice sentence became the object of the dative preposition ***von*** in the passive voice sentence and had no effect on the conjugated verb: ***von dem Professor***. Since the tense of the active sentence was the simple past tense, the same tense was used in the passive voice sentence.

Now let's look at a passive sentence in all its tenses:

PRESENT
Das Haus wird von dem Feind zerstört.

The house is being destroyed by the enemy.

PAST
Das Haus wurde von dem Feind zerstört.

The house was destroyed by the enemy.

PRESENT PERFECT
Das Haus ist von dem Feind zerstört worden.

The house has been destroyed by the enemy.

PAST PERFECT
Das Haus war von dem Feind zerstört worden.

The house had been destroyed by the enemy.

FUTURE
Das Haus wird von dem Feind zerstört werden.

The house will be destroyed by the enemy.

FUTURE PERFECT
Das Haus wird von dem Feind zerstört worden sein.

The house will have been destroyed by the enemy.

Note: There is a tendency to avoid the future perfect in the passive voice.

Careful! Do not confuse ***worden*** and ***geworden***. The participle ***worden*** is used exclusively in the passive voice as the past participle: ***Ich bin gefragt worden***. The participle ***geworden*** is from the verb *to become* and is not used in the passive voice: ***Mein Bruder ist Lehrer geworden***.

Remember that the tense of the active sentence must be the tense of the passive sentence as well:

PRESENT
*Karl **bringt** die Bilder.*   Karl brings the pictures.
*Die Bilder **werden** von Karl*   The pictures are being brought
  gebracht.   by Karl.

PRESENT PERFECT
*Karl **hat** die Bilder **gebracht**.*   Karl has brought the pictures.
*Die Bilder **sind** von Karl gebracht*   The pictures have been brought
  ***worden**.*   by Karl.

The active sentence above had a direct object (***die Bilder***), which became the subject of the passive sentence. But remember that German also has dative verbs. It is possible for active sentences with dative verbs to be changed to the passive voice. However, this can only occur with dative verbs that are **not verbs of motion** or **intransitive**. Dative verbs of motion are identified by the use of ***sein*** as their auxiliary in the perfect tenses.

DATIVE VERB
*Die Jungen **haben** ihr **geholfen**.*   The boys have helped her.

DATIVE VERB OF MOTION
*Der Hund **ist** ihr **entlaufen**.*   The dog has run away from her.

DATIVE VERB
*Sie **hat** uns **gedient**.*   She has served us.

INTRANSITIVE DATIVE VERB
*Es **ist** ihm nicht **gelungen**.*   He hasn't succeeded.

When an active sentence with a dative verb is changed to the passive, the dative object **remains in the dative case**. The subject of the passive sentence becomes the elliptical word ***es***; that is, the verb ***werden*** is conjugated in the third person singular, but the subject is not shown in the sentence. Notice how the active voice is changed to the passive voice with a dative verb.

ACTIVE VOICE—DATIVE VERB
Sie helfen ihr.   They are helping her.
Er drohte den Bauern.   He threatened the farmers.

PASSIVE VOICE—DATIVE VERB

Ihr wird geholfen.	She is being helped.
Den Bauern wurde gedroht.	The farmers were threatened.

Now let's look at the active voice and the passive voice of a dative verb in all the tenses. Remember that the tense of the active voice sentence must be the same tense as the passive voice sentence in order for them to be counterparts of one another:

PRESENT

Sie danken dem Gastgeber für den Empfang.	They thank the host for the reception.
Dem Gastgeber wird für den Empfang gedankt.	The host is thanked for the reception.

PAST

Sie dankten dem Gastgeber für den Empfang.	They thanked the host for the reception.
Dem Gastgeber wurde für den Empfang gedankt.	The host was thanked for the reception.

PRESENT PERFECT

Sie haben dem Gastgeber für den Empfang gedankt.	They have thanked the host for the reception.
Dem Gastgeber ist für den Empfang gedankt worden.	The host has been thanked for the reception.

PAST PERFECT

Sie hatten dem Gastgeber für den Empfang gedankt.	They had thanked the host for the reception.
Dem Gastgeber war für den Empfang gedankt worden.	The host had been thanked for the reception.

FUTURE

Sie werden dem Gastgeber für den Empfang danken.	They will thank the host for the reception.
Dem Gastgeber wird für den Empfang gedankt werden.	The host will be thanked for the reception.

FUTURE PERFECT

Sie werden dem Gastgeber für den Empfang gedankt haben.	They will have thanked the host for the reception.
Dem Gastgeber wird für den Empfang gedankt worden sein.	The host will have been thanked for the reception.

Modal auxiliaries can be used in the passive voice but must be followed by a passive voice infinitive, which in English looks like this: *to be understood, to be found, to be learned,* and so forth.

This problem **can be understood** better if we examine it from another point of view.

The treasure **must be found** before the break of dawn.

This concept **should be learned** before one goes on to the next one.

And, of course, the modals can appear in various tenses.

Modal auxiliaries in German passive voice sentences act in the same way. A modal auxiliary is followed by a passive voice infinitive: ***gefunden werden, verhaftet werden, gelernt werden***, and so on. And the modal auxiliaries used with passive voice infinitives can occur in various tenses.

First, let's look at a few of the modals in the present tense:

*Das **darf** nicht gemacht werden.*	That cannot be done.
***Kann** der Mann wirklich verhaftet werden?*	Can the man really be arrested?
*Die verlorenen Bücher **müssen** gefunden werden.*	The lost books have to be found.

Now look at a passive voice sentence with the modal ***müssen*** in all the tenses:

PRESENT

Der ganze Roman muss gelesen werden.	The entire novel has to be read.

PAST

Der ganze Roman musste gelesen werden.	The entire novel had to be read.

PRESENT PERFECT

Der ganze Roman hat gelesen
  werden müssen.

The entire novel has had to be
  read.

PAST PERFECT

Der ganze Roman hatte gelesen
  werden müssen.

The entire novel had had to be
  read.

FUTURE

Der ganze Roman wird gelesen
  werden müssen.

The entire novel will have to be
  read.

The addition of a modal auxiliary to a passive voice sentence is not such an enormous complication. It is really just like the simple usage of a modal auxiliary with a single infinitive. It's just that in the passive voice the infinitive is made up of a past participle and **werden**.

SINGLE INFINITIVE

*Er kann es nicht **verstehen**.*

He cannot understand it.

PASSIVE INFINITIVE

*Es kann nicht **verstanden**
  werden.*

It cannot be understood.

The German passive voice is an important structure. It is widely used and acceptable as good style.

Exercise 1

Rewrite the following verbs as passive infinitives. For example:

sehen gesehen werden

1. versprechen _____

2. töten _____

3. ausschließen _____

4. annehmen _____

5. zeigen _____

6. verlernen _____

7. behalten _____

8. komponieren _____

Exercise 2

Rewrite the present tense passive sentences in the past, present perfect, and future tenses.

1. Ein Haus wird gebaut.

_____.

_____.

_____.

2. Die Kinder werden von einem neuen Lehrer unterrichtet.

_____.

_____.

_____.

3. Ihm wird damit geholfen.

_____.

_____.

_____.

4. Wirst du verhaftet?

_____ .

_____ .

_____ .

Exercise 3

Rewrite each active sentence as a passive sentence. Retain the original tense of the active sentence.

1. Der Student besucht eine neue Ausstellung.

_____ .

2. Die Kellnerin brachte einen Teller Suppe.

_____ .

3. Goethe hat Dramen und Gedichte geschrieben.

_____ .

4. Sie haben ihnen herzlich gedankt.

_____ .

5. Wir werden die neuen Wörter lernen.

_____ .

15

The Subjunctive Mood

The subjunctive mood in English seems to be a dying form. Many English speakers merely substitute a past tense conjugation where traditionally a subjunctive conjugation is required. For example, you will often hear:

I wish he **was** here.

Traditionally, that sentence should be stated as:

I wish he **were** here.

English speakers are deciding that they do not need subjunctive forms to communicate, so this conjugational form may die out completely in the next generation or two unless the English-speaking world has a sudden change of heart. Certain pat phrases in the subjunctive survive, but most English speakers do not even realize that the verbs in those phrases are conjugated in the subjunctive:

Be that as it **may**.
Long **live** the king!
Be he beggar or **be** he king.

While the subjunctive mood is quickly losing ground in modern English, this is not the case in German. In German, there are special complexities to consider when addressing the subjunctive mood. First of all, remember that there are three types of subjunctive conjugations: one that is formed from the infinitive of the verb, **subjunctive I** (often called the present subjunctive conjugation); one that is formed from the past tense of the verb, **subjunctive II** (often called the past subjunctive conjugation); and the **conditional** conjugation. Let's take a look at those conjugational forms in the third person singular:

PRESENT SUBJUNCTIVE CONJUGATION (I)

fragen	*haben*	*sein*
er frage	*er habe*	*er sei*
er habe gefragt	*er habe gehabt*	*er sei gewesen*
er werde fragen	*er werde haben*	*er werde sein*

The subjunctive I conjugations are formed from a verb's stem (the infinitive minus the **-en** ending) with the endings **-e**, **-est**, **-e**, **-en**, **-et**, and **-en**. The only exception is the verb **sein**.

Now let's look at the past subjunctive conjugation (II) in the third person singular:

PAST SUBJUNCTIVE CONJUGATION (II)

fragen	*haben*	*sein*
er fragte	*er hätte*	*er wäre*
er hätte gefragt	*er hätte gehabt*	*er wäre gewesen*
er würde fragen	*er würde haben*	*er würde sein*

The subjunctive II conjugation of regular verbs looks like the simple past tense: for example, **sagte**, **sagtest**, **sagte**, **sagten**, **sagtet**, and **sagten** are the forms for both the indicative past and the subjunctive II of the verb **sagen**. Irregular verbs are another story. After forming the irregular past tense, use the endings **-e**, **-est**, **-e**, **-en**, **-et**, and **-en**. If the verb has the vowel **a**, **o**, or, **u**, add an umlaut (i.e., **ä**, **ö**, **ü**).For example, since **haben** has an **a**, you would add an umlaut: **hätte**, **hättest**, **hätte**, **hätten**, **hättet,** and **hätten**.

Note that in subjunctive II, an umlaut is added to a modal auxiliary only if the modal has an umlaut in its infinitive:

Modal Auxiliary	*Past Tense*	*Subjunctive II*
dürfen	*durfte*	*dürfte*
können	*konnte*	*könnte*

mögen	*mochte*	*möchte*
müssen	*musste*	*müsste*
sollen	*sollte*	*sollte*
wollen	*wollte*	*wollte*

Now let's look at the conditional conjugation in the third person singular:

CONDITIONAL
er würde fragen   *er würde haben*   *er würde sein*
er würde gefragt haben   *er würde gehabt haben*   *er würde gewesen sein*

The conditional conjugation is formed from the subjunctive II conjugation of **werden** (**würde**, **würdest**, **würde**, **würden**, **würdet**, and **würden**) followed by an infinitive.

After you are familiar with the subjunctive conjugational patterns, it is time to look at their applications. An important application of the present subjunctive conjugation is in **indirect discourse**.

Indirect Discourse
Direct discourse is the exact quote of someone's words:

The foreman said, "The workers need more time."

Indirect discourse is the retelling of that quote to someone else:

The foreman said that the workers need more time.

Note that the quotation marks are gone and the word *that* has been added. (The word *that* is optional.) This is no longer a direct quote; it is no longer direct discourse. It is indirect discourse, and in German indirect discourse requires the conjugated verb to be in the present subjunctive (subjunctive I). Let's look at some examples of statements that **der Lehrling** (the apprentice) made:

DIRECT DISCOURSE

Der Lehrling sagte, „Sie hat keine Zeit dazu.“

The apprentice said, "She doesn't have any time for that."

INDIRECT DISCOURSE

*Der Lehrling sagte, dass er keine Zeit dazu **habe**. or*

*Der Lehrling sagte, er **habe** keine Zeit dazu.*

The apprentice said he doesn't have any time for that.

DIRECT DISCOURSE

Der Lehrling sagte, „Die Arbeiter sind nach Hause gegangen.“

The apprentice said, "The workers have gone home."

INDIRECT DISCOURSE

*Der Lehrling sagte, dass die Arbeiter nach Hause gegangen **seien**. or*

*Der Lehrling sagte, die Arbeiter **seien** nach Hause gegangen.*

The apprentice said the workers have gone home.

In indirect discourse it is optional to use the conjunction ***dass*** to combine the two parts of the sentence. Using ***dass*** requires the conjugated verb to be the last element in the clause.

If the present subjunctive conjugation is identical to the indicative, you should use the past subjunctive conjugation.

DIRECT DISCOURSE

Der Lehrling sagte, „Die Arbeiter haben keine Zeit dazu.“

The apprentice said, "The workers don't have any time for that."

INDIRECT DISCOURSE

*Der Lehrling sagte, dass die Arbeiter keine Zeit dazu **hätten**. or*

*Der Lehrling sagte, die Arbeiter **hätten** keine Zeit dazu.*

The apprentice said the workers don't have any time for that.

Compare the indicative conjugation with the present subjunctive conjugation. When they are identical, switch to the past subjunctive conjugation as is demonstrated in the example above.

Indicative	*Present Subj.*	*Change to Past Subj.*
ich habe	*ich habe*	*ich hätte*
du hast	*du habest*	
er hat	*er habe*	
wir haben	*wir haben*	*wir hätten*
ihr habt	*ihr habet*	
sie haben	*sie haben*	*sie hätten*

The same rules apply for changing a direct question to an indirect question:

DIRECT QUESTION
Der Mann fragte, „Wer singt so schön?"

The man asked, "Who is singing so beautifully?"

INDIRECT QUESTION
Der Mann fragte, wer so schön **singe**.

The man asked who is singing so beautifully.

If there is no interrogative word (**wer**, **was**, **wo**, **wann**, etc.) to combine the two parts of the sentence, use **ob**:

DIRECT QUESTION
Ihre Freundin fragte, „Will sie diese Bluse verkaufen?"

Her friend asked, "Does she want to sell this blouse?"

INDIRECT QUESTION
Ihre Freundin fragte, ob sie diese Bluse verkaufen **wolle**.

Her friend asked whether she wants to sell this blouse.

And, again, if the indicative and present subjunctive are identical, change to the past subjunctive:

DIRECT QUESTION

Der Mann fragte, „Wie können sie   The man asked, "What is the
ihr Haus am besten verkaufen?"   best way to sell their house?"

INDIRECT QUESTION

Der Mann fragte, wie sie ihr Haus   The man asked what the best
*am besten verkaufen **könnten**.*   way is to sell their house.

Indicative	Present Subj.	Change to Past Subj.
ich kann	ich könne	
du kannst	du könnest	
er kann	er könne	
wir können	wir können	wir könnten
ihr könnt	ihr könnet	
sie können	sie können	sie könnten

If you are going to change a past tense statement that is direct discourse to indirect discourse, you have to form the subjunctive verb like the present perfect tense.

DIRECT DISCOURSE

*Mutter sagte, „Mein Bruder **war***   Mother said, "My brother was at
beim Zahnarzt."   the dentist."

INDIRECT DISCOURSE

Mutter sagte, dass ihr Bruder beim   Mother said that her brother was
*Zahnarzt **gewesen sei**. or*   at the dentist's.
*Mutter sagte, ihr Bruder **sei** beim*
*Zahnarzt **gewesen**.*

DIRECT QUESTION

*Mutter fragte, „**Besuchte** Onkel*   Mother asked, "Did Uncle
Friedrich das Museum?"   Friedrich visit the museum?"

INDIRECT QUESTION

Mutter fragte, ob Onkel Friedrich   Mother asked whether Uncle
*das Museum **besucht habe**.*   Friedrich visited the museum.

In the spoken language, there is a tendency for Germans to use the past subjunctive conjugation in place of the present subjunctive conjugation in indirect discourse. The present subjunctive conjugation sounds more academic and is used for literary language. The past subjunctive conjugation sounds more casual.

WRITTEN GERMAN

*Die Richterin sagte, er **sei** schuldig.*	The judge said he is guilty.
*Die Richterin sagte, er **sei** schuldig* ***gewesen**.*	The judge said he was guilty.

SPOKEN GERMAN

*Die Richterin hat gesagt, er **wäre** schuldig.*	The judge said he is guilty.
*Die Richterin hat gesagt, er **wäre** schuldig **gewesen**.*	The judge said he was guilty.

Remember, too, that the past tense is usually expressed by the present perfect tense in casual speech. The simple past tense is more frequently a written form and used for narratives. Thus, in the above sentence ***hat gesagt*** is used in the spoken version, not ***sagte***.

Als ob (*als wenn*)

The past subjunctive conjugation is also used after the conjunction ***als ob*** (or ***als wenn***), which means *as if*. This conjunction requires the conjugated verb to be placed at the end of the ***als ob*** clause.

*Er tat so, als ob er jetzt ein reicher Mann **wäre**.*	He acted as if he were a rich man now.
*Die Frau weinte, als ob sie keine Hoffnung mehr **hätte**.*	The woman cried as if she had no more hope.
*Das Mädchen lächelte, als ob der Junge eine Dummheit **gesagt hätte**.*	The girl smiled as if the boy had said something stupid.
*Karl sprach, als ob sein eigener Bruder sein ärgster Feind **geworden wäre**.*	Karl spoke as if his own brother had become his worst enemy.

Special verbal structures such as dative verbs or the passive voice have no influence on subjunctive voice conjugations:

Die Frau tat so, als ob sie mir **helfen** *könnte.*	The woman acted as if she could help me.
Das Kind schrie, als ob es von seinem Vater **verprügelt worden** *wäre.*	The child screamed as if he had been beaten by his father.

Wenn

The past subjunctive conjugation is used with the conjunction **wenn**, which, when used with the subjunctive mood, means *if*. This conjunction does not require the past subjunctive when it means *when*:

Wenn *ich in Berlin bin, besuche ich meine Verwandten.*	**When** I'm in Berlin, I visit my relatives.

Use the past subjunctive only when **wenn** means *if*:

Wenn *ich doch wieder in Berlin* **wäre!**	**If** only I were back in Berlin.

Sometimes there is only a single **wenn** clause to express an emotional idea, such as in the above example. It is also possible to express the same kind of emotional idea with the omission of the conjunction **wenn**. This can be done by placing the conjugated verb at the beginning of the sentence:

Wenn *du doch deine Familie nie verlassen* **hättest!**	If only you had never left your family.

or

Hättest *du doch deine Familie nie verlassen!*

With specific wishes, the same kind of past subjunctive conjugation is required. Often the two parts of the sentence are combined by the conjunction **dass**.

| *Ich **wünschte**, dass ich wieder gesund wäre!* | I wish I were well again. |
| *Ich **wollte**, dass ich mehr Glück hätte!* | I wish I had more luck. |

Using the conjunction ***dass*** is optional and can be omitted in both the written and spoken language.

| *Ich **wünschte**, ich könnte Ihnen helfen!* | I wish I could help you. |
| *Ich **wollte**, ich hätte besser gesungen!* | I wish I had sung better. |

Notice that these emotional or wish statements all end with an exclamation point. And in wish statements, take note that the verbs ***wünschen*** and ***wollen*** are conjugated in the past subjunctive.

The English conjunction *if* is used to combine two sentences into one. When this occurs, the verbs in the sentences change to the subjunctive mood:

| My friend is here. I am happy. | **If** my friend were here, I would be happy. |
| She laughs. She sees this clown. | She would laugh **if** she saw this clown. |

Sentences like these with an *if* clause suggest a hypothetical meaning: *My hypothesis is that I would be happy,* if my friend were here. Or this kind of structure sets a **condition** that could determine a **certain result**.

If my friend were here, I would be happy.
Condition: If my friend were here.
Result: I would be happy.

She would laugh if she saw this clown.
Condition: If she saw this clown.
Result: She would laugh.

This kind of hypothetical or conditional statement also occurs in German. The conjunction ***wenn*** is used to combine two sentences into one, and the two clauses that are formed both require the verbs to be conjugated in the past subjunctive. The result is a hypothetical or conditional statement. Once again, it is optional to omit the conjunction **wenn** when it introduces the sentence.

TWO SENTENCES

Bonn ist näher. Wir fahren dorthin.   Bonn is nearer. We drive there.

COMBINED BY *WENN*

Wenn *Bonn näher wäre, würden*   If Bonn were nearer, we would
  wir dorthin fahren. or   drive there.
Wäre Bonn näher, würden wir
  dorthin fahren. or
Wenn *Bonn näher wäre, führen*
  wir dorthin.

Condition: *Wenn Bonn näher wäre.*
Result: *Würden wir dorthin fahren.*

In the following example, **wenn** is used to introduce the second clause. It is not an option to omit **wenn** when it occurs in this part of the sentence.

TWO SENTENCES

Die Firma entlässt ihn. Er arbeitet   The company fires him. He
  schlecht.   works badly.

COMBINED BY *WENN*

Die Firma würde ihn entlassen,   The company would fire him if
  wenn *er schlecht arbeitete.* or   he worked badly.
Die Firma entließe ihn, **wenn** *er*
  schlecht arbeitete.

Condition: *Wenn er schlecht arbeitete.*
Result: *Die Firma würde ihn entlassen.*

If the two original sentences are in the past tense or the present perfect tense, the past subjunctive conjugation of the present perfect tense is used in the combined sentence.

TWO SENTENCES

Die Firma entließ ihn. Er arbeitete schlecht.	The company fired him. He worked badly.

COMBINED BY *WENN*

Die Firma würde ihn entlassen haben, **wenn** *er schlecht gearbeitet hätte.* or *Die Firma hätte ihn entlassen,* **wenn** *er schlecht gearbeitet hätte.*	The company would have fired him if he had worked badly.

TWO SENTENCES

Bonn ist näher gewesen. Wir sind dorthin gefahren.	Bonn was nearer. We drove there.

COMBINED BY *WENN*

Wenn *Bonn näher gewesen wäre, würden wir dorthin gefahren sein.* or *Wäre Bonn näher gewesen, wären wir dorthin gefahren.* or **Wenn** *Bonn näher gewesen wäre, wären wir dorthin gefahren.*	If Bonn had been nearer, we would have driven there.

There is a tendency to use the less complicated forms in structures like these. Therefore, ***wären wir dorthin gefahren*** is preferable to ***würden wir dorthin gefahren sein***. You should be aware, however, that both conjugational forms exist.

The non-***wenn*** clause can begin with the word ***so*** or ***dann***. This is optional and is the choice of the speaker or writer. Note that this can only occur if the sentence begins with the conjunction ***wenn***. If ***so*** or ***dann*** is used, the conjugated verb follows.

Wenn Bonn näher wäre, **so** *würden wir dorthin fahren.*
Wenn er schlecht gearbeitet hätte, **dann** *hätte die Firma ihn entlassen.*

When there is a single verb in each clause of sentences that are combined by ***wenn***, it is possible to conjugate the verb in the past subjunctive or to connect them to the verb ***würden***. The meaning is the same in both forms; this is true even when *wenn* is omitted but understood, as in the second example:

Bonn ist näher. Wir fahren dorthin.
*Wäre Bonn näher, **würden** wir dorthin **fahren**.*
*Wenn Bonn näher wäre, **führen** wir dorthin.*

There are times when *würden* is found in both clauses, even the *wenn* clause. There is a tendency to use *würden* in a *wenn* clause if the verb is not a high-frequency verb (i.e., not *kommen*, *gehen*, *sein*, *haben*, etc.) and if it has a regular conjugation.

*Wenn ich das Gedicht auswendig lernen **würde**, würde ich einen Preis gewinnen.*	If I would learn the poem by heart, I would win a prize.

Careful! There are times when English uses *would* in certain expressions that look like the subjunctive. The tendency is to form a subjunctive with *würden* in German as the translation. But the English use of *would* is sometimes only a little additive in sentences to suggest an action or activity that is a habit or done frequently. Consider the meaning of these sentences:

I would lie in bed for hours and think about space travel.
Where would you shop when you spent the summer at the lake?
She would call me all kinds of names and then burst into tears.

Despite the use of the verb *would*, the verbs in these sentences cannot be conjugated in German in the subjunctive mood. They are expressions of habit or frequency. Compare them to the following sentences:

I often lay in bed for hours and thought about space travel.
Where did you shop when you spent summers at the lake?
She frequently called me all kinds of names and then burst into tears.

Notice how German expresses similar ideas.

Sie hat oft mit den Kindern gespielt.	She would often play with the children.

Ich bin immer gerade nach Hause gegangen.   I would always go straight home.

Wenn es regnete, blieben sie zu Hause.   Whenever it rained, they would stay home.

Ich möchte

Another expression that requires a little more examination has to do with using the verb *would* to make a statement or question sound more polite. The phrase *would like* can replace *want* in a sentence and make it sound less abrupt.

> Yes, we **want** some cake. (abrupt)
> Yes, we **would like** some cake. (polite)
> I **want** to stay home. (abrupt)
> I **would like** to stay home. (polite)

Notice that these expressions are used both with objects (*some cake*) and verbs (*to stay*).

Interestingly, German has the same expressions and usage. The modal auxiliary **wollen** is a high-frequency verb but expresses the desire for something abruptly. It may not sound completely impolite to say *ich will etwas*, but that phrase would probably be used more often among close friends than with others. The German equivalent for the English phrase *would like* is the past subjunctive of **mögen**:

ich möchte	*wir möchten*
du möchtest	*ihr möchtet*
er, sie, es möchte	*sie möchten*
Sie möchten	

It is used in place of **wollen** to make a statement sound less abrupt and to be polite:

*Ich **will** ein Stück Kuchen.* (abrupt)
*Ich **möchte** ein Stück Kuchen.*   I'd like a piece of cake.
   (polite)

Willst du mitkommen? (abrupt)
Möchten Sie mitkommen? (polite)   Would you like to come along?

Although English speakers may not always have a practical need for the subjunctive mood and can communicate adequately without it, it is still a form that exists in the language and that must be given consideration. Perhaps this consideration is needed if only to understand the English subjunctive voice in order to better understand the German subjunctive voice.

You have learned that in German there are various applications of the subjunctive and they play an important role in the language.

• The subjunctive is needed to express indirect discourse:

Die Krankenschwester berichtete,   The nurse reported that the
  dem Kranken gehe es wieder viel   patient is doing much better
  besser.   again.

• The subjunctive is used to make an emotional statement:

Hätte ich doch meine Tasche nicht   If only I hadn't forgotten my
  vergessen!   purse.

• The subjunctive expresses a wish:

Ich wünschte, dass ich wieder in   I wish I were in Germany again.
  Deutschland wäre.

• The subjunctive is used in clauses that follow *als ob* (*als wenn*):

Er tat so, als wenn er nicht   He acted as if he couldn't
  verstehen könnte.   understand.

• The subjunctive conjugation is used in two clauses combined by **wenn**:

Wenn es nicht genug regnete,   If it didn't rain enough, the earth
  würde die Erde trocken werden.   would become dry.

• The subjunctive is used to make an expression of want or desire sound more polite:

Ich möchte Spiegeleier bitte.　　　　I'd like fried eggs please.

A few high-frequency verbs form their past tense subjunctive according to an older form. The list is not long, but you should be aware of this irregularity. In some cases, both the older form and the standard approach to forming the past tense subjunctive are acceptable.

Infinitive	*Past Subjunctive*	*Acceptable Form*
helfen	*hülfe*	*hälfe*
stehen	*stünde*	*stände*
sterben	*stürbe*	N/A
verderben	*verdürbe*	N/A
werfen	*würfe*	N/A

There are other verbs that also have two forms for the past tense subjunctive. Check the appendix in your dictionary for other verbs that do not always form this structure in the standard way.

Exercise 1

Rewrite the infinitives below in the present subjunctive and the past subjunctive with the pronoun *er*.

1. schließen _____

2. ankommen _____

3. sich benehmen _____

4. kaufen _____

5. imponieren _____

6. vergessen _____

7. beschreiben _____

8. durchlesen _____

9. zerstören _____

10. sein _____

Exercise 2

Write the statements in direct discourse as indirect discourse. Begin each one with **Der Mann sagte, dass** . . .

1. „Karl ruhte sich an keinem einzigen Sonntag aus."

_____.

2. „Man baut hier viele Häuser aus Holz."

_____.

3. „Die Schweizer lieben die Alpen."

_____.

4. „Seine Kinder sind ungeschickt."

_____.

5. „Der Professor saß stundenlang über seinen Büchern."

_____.

Exercise 3

Complete the phrase ***Er tat so, als ob*** . . . with each of the sentences provided. For example:

Er ist ein König.
Er tat so, als ob er ein König wäre.

1. Er hat mich nicht gesehen.

   _____.

2. Seine Frau ist eine Schönheitskönigin.

   _____.

3. Er ist sehr reich geworden.

   _____.

4. Er verheiratete sich mit einer Schauspielerin.

   _____.

Exercise 4

Complete each sentence with the given phrase.

1. Sie hat nicht gearbeitet.

Wenn _____, hätte sie kein Geld verdient.

2. Ich habe Flügel.

Wenn _____, würde ich wie ein Vogel fliegen.

3. Vater ist wieder gesund gewesen.

Wenn _____, hätte er nach Hause gehen dürfen.

4. Karl sprach gut Deutsch.

Wenn _____, hätte er die Rede auf deutsch

gehalten.

5. Er schreibt mir oft.

Wenn er mehr Zeit hätte, _____.

6. Ich erkenne ihn sofort.

Wenn mein alter Freund mich besuchte, _____.

7. Sie hat keine Fragen mehr.

Wenn sie das wüsste, _____.

8. Ich kann alles lesen.

Wenn ich eine neue Brille hätte, _____.

Exercise 5

Combine the following pairs of sentences with **wenn**. The clause that sets
the condition should begin with **wenn**.

1. Wir haben ihn eingeladen. Er ist ein freundlicher Mensch

gewesen.

_____.

2. Ich habe das gesagt. Ich habe das gemeint.

_____.

3. Er kann reisen. Er besucht die Türkei.

_____.

4. Die Arbeiter spielen Schach. Sie haben mehr Freizeit.

_____.

5. Sie ist nicht so gemein gewesen. Sie hat mich wirklich geliebt.

_____.

Verbs Ending in *-ieren*

Cognates are words that have the same appearance and function in two or more languages. In the case of European languages, cognates tend to be words that come from a Latin or Greek source. Even if those words were invented in a modern time by putting together two or more Latin or Greek words, they are still considered cognates. Look at these examples:

polygraph—phonograph—photograph
television—telegraph—telephone

These words are cognates but became part of European—and even some non-European—languages only recently.

There are other words that are common to both English and German (and some other European languages) that could also be called cognates. Often they are identical in English and German. And in some cases there is only a slight variance between the two languages. Some of the words are old. Some come from a very recent time. Here are just a few:

English	*German*
address	*Adresse*
club	*Club*
film	*Film*
innovative	*innovativ*

The point being made is that the task of learning German if you are an English speaker, or of learning English if you are a German speaker, is made much easier by the fact that a large amount of vocabulary can become yours almost immediately because the two languages share so many words in common. It is really a matter of pronunciation and, in the case of the German language, knowing the gender of the cognate nouns that cause any consternation.

There is also a category of verbs that lends itself to quick study—verbs that end in *-ieren*. Most verbs that end in *-ieren* are foreign words that have been adapted for German. They always have a regular conjugation, and depending upon whether they are transitive or intransitive, their auxiliary in the perfect tenses can be **haben** or **sein**. In the perfect tenses the participle never has the prefix **ge-** (e.g., **er hat studiert** = *he has studied* and **er ist spaziert** = *he has strolled*).

Verbs that end in *-ieren* are very practical for the student of German: They have a regular conjugation that is easy to apply, and their English meaning is, for the most part, immediately understandable.

Care must be taken, however, when using a verb that ends in *-ieren*. On occasion, the meaning you require may not be as obvious as you think. You may need a different verb from the one you have in mind because there are often numerous meanings to an English verb. For example, consider the English verb *fix*. There is more than one meaning for this little word and one of them is translated into German as **fixieren**. Let's assume that you want to use this verb to tell your German mechanic that you need your transmission *fixed* and wonder if this is the appropriate verb for what you want to communicate. We now need to take a close look at **fixieren** and a couple other verbs as well. All three of the following verbs mean *to fix* but have a specific meaning and use:

befestigen	to fix, fasten, or attach to something
fixieren	to fix one's eyes on something
reparieren	to fix, mend, or repair something

Is **fixieren** really the verb needed to tell your mechanic that you want your transmission *fixed*? The answer is obvious and is evidence that you cannot rush when choosing a verb ending in *-ieren* just because it looks like what you want.

The same is true if you start with the German verb and assume it has the same meaning as the English verb it looks like. For example, you may come upon the verb *installieren,* and you wish to say *install* in a certain context. But for certain ideas *installieren* is not the appropriate verb. Consider the following sentence:

Er hat neue Schränke in der Küche   He installed new cupboards in
   eingebaut.   the kitchen.

The idea of *to install* in the above sentence has to do with building the cupboards into the kitchen complex. The verb *einbauen* is, therefore, preferable. *Installieren* would be more appropriate for installing software.

The verb *probieren* provides another example. If you want to use the verb *probieren* and believe that it is related to the English word *probe,* you will come up with a sentence that will make little sense in German. *Probieren* is related to the German word *die Probe,* which means a *test, trial,* or *experiment.* Look at this verb used in a sentence:

Der junge Mann hat den schönen   The young man wanted to try
   *Apfelkuchen **probieren** wollen.*   the beautiful apple cake.

The meaning of *probieren* is *try* or *taste* and has little to do with the English word *probe,* which has as one of its meanings *to explore a cavity with an instrument.*

What does this mean for English speakers? Always check in a dictionary for the special uses of verbs; verbs ending in *-ieren* are no exception even though they look so straightforward. The first entry in a dictionary definition is not necessarily the appropriate one for the meaning you wish to impart. You have to check all the entries to find the appropriate one for your needs.

The verbs *arrangieren* and *compilieren,* for example, look like *arrange* and *compile.* And that is their meaning in German.

Sie haben einen großen Empfang   They arranged a big reception.
   arrangiert.

Er soll das Computerprogramm   He should compile the computer
   jetzt compilieren.   program now.

In most dictionaries you will find *compilieren* spelled *kompilieren*. The spelling *compilieren* is a modern twist and popular among computer users.

English speakers cannot become complacent about *-ieren* verbs. These verbs must always be checked for their exact meaning. For example, the verb *dressieren* may remind you of *dress*, and the verb *spionieren* may not give you a clue at all as to its meaning. In both cases, English speakers must learn new meanings for these verbs:

Diese großen Hunde waren auf den Mann dressiert.	These large dogs were trained to go after people.
Die alte Dame hatte für den Feind spioniert.	The old lady had spied for the enemy.

It is important to distinguish between those verbs ending in *-ieren* that have the same meaning as English verbs and those that merely look somewhat like English verbs. Since verbs in this category are so comfortable to use, students of German are sometimes eager to presume that they have found the appropriate word for their purposes. But caution is required. Always check a dictionary for the precise meaning and usage of a verb ending in *-ieren*.

Also be aware that there are several German verbs that end in *-ieren* that do not belong in this category at all. They are true German verbs and do not come from a foreign source. They merely share the same *look* as *-ieren* verbs. Look at the infinitive, meaning, and principal parts of the following three verbs. From the principal parts you can see that these are not *-ieren* verbs:

frieren	freeze	*er friert, er fror, er hat gefroren, er wird frieren*
verlieren	lose	*er verliert, er verlor, er hat verloren, er wird verlieren*
zieren	adorn	*er ziert, er zierte, er hat geziert, er wird zieren*

Exercise 1
Write original sentences with the following verbs that end in *-ieren*.

1. studieren

_____.

2. imitieren

_____.

3. imponieren

_____.

4. organisieren

_____.

5. sich rasieren

_____.

Exercise 2
Check a dictionary and write the most prominent definition for each of the following words. Consider what the verbs *look like* and what they *really mean*.

1. spendieren _____

2. photographieren _____

3. möblieren _____

4. garnieren _____

5. hantieren _____

6. isolieren _____

7. magnetisieren _____

8. galvanisieren _____

9. mobilisieren _____

10. filtrieren _____

Exercise 3

Rewrite each present tense sentence in the past, the present perfect, and the future tenses.

1. Die Arbeiter demonstrieren vor dem Rathaus.

_____ .

_____ .

_____ .

2. Der Knabe verliert seinen Hut.

_____ .

_____ .

_____ .

Quick-Glance Tables

Commonly Used Reflexive Verbs

The following list contains commonly used accusative and dative reflexive verbs and transitive verbs that are frequently used with a reflexive. For example, consider the transitive verb *fragen*: *Ich **frage** die Frau* or *Ich **frage** mich*.

Infinitive	English	Accusative	Dative
sich ändern	to change	✓	
sich anziehen	to dress	✓	✓
sich ärgern	to annoy	✓	
sich ausdrücken	to express oneself	✓	
sich ausziehen	to undress	✓	✓
sich bedanken	to thank	✓	
sich beeilen	to hurry	✓	
sich befinden	to be located	✓	
sich benehmen	to behave	✓	
sich beschweren	to complain	✓	
sich bewegen	to move	✓	
sich denken	to imagine		✓
sich drehen	to turn	✓	
sich einbilden	to imagine		✓
sich erinnern	to remember	✓	
sich erkälten	to catch cold	✓	
sich fragen	to ask	✓	

Infinitive	English	Accusative	Dative
sich freuen	to be glad	✓	
sich fühlen	to feel	✓	
sich fürchten	to fear	✓	
sich helfen	to help oneself		✓
sich interessieren	to be interested	✓	
sich irren	to be wrong	✓	
sich kämmen	to comb one's hair		✓
sich kümmern	to care about	✓	
sich legen	to lie down	✓	
sich nähern	to approach		✓
sich setzen	to take a seat	✓	
sich stellen	to place oneself	✓	
sich treffen	to meet up	✓	
sich überzeugen	to convince	✓	
sich umziehen	to change clothes	✓	✓
sich unterhalten	to converse	✓	
sich verzeihen	to forgive oneself		✓
sich vorstellen	to introduce oneself	✓	
sich vorstellen	to imagine		✓
sich waschen	to wash	✓	✓
sich widersprechen	to contradict oneself		✓

Verbs, Auxiliaries, and Their Functions

Use this listing of verbs as a quick check of the auxiliary required for each verb and the function or reason for that auxiliary type. This list contains high-frequency verbs, many with either a separable or inseparable prefix.

Infinitive	Trans.	Intrans.	Haben	Sein	Verb of Motion	Radical Change	Dative Verb
anrufen	✓		✓				
antworten	✓		✓				✓
aufstehen		✓		✓	✓		
austrinken	✓		✓				

Infinitive	Trans.	Intrans.	Haben	Sein	Verb of Motion	Radical Change	Dative Verb
backen	✓		✓				
beantworten	✓		✓				
befehlen		✓	✓				✓
begegnen		✓		✓			✓
beissen	✓		✓				
sich benehmen	✓		✓				
beschreiben	✓		✓				
bitten	✓		✓				
bleiben		✓		✓		✓	
brechen	✓		✓				
bringen	✓		✓				
danken		✓	✓				✓
denken	✓		✓				
dienen		✓	✓				✓
einschlafen		✓		✓			✓
empfangen	✓		✓				
entkommen		✓		✓	✓		✓
entlaufen		✓		✓	✓		✓
erschlagen	✓		✓				
erwarten	✓		✓				
essen	✓		✓				
fahren		✓		✓	✓		
fallen		✓		✓	✓		
finden	✓		✓				
fliegen		✓		✓	✓		
folgen		✓		✓	✓		✓
fragen	✓		✓				
frieren		✓		✓		✓	
geben	✓		✓				
gehen		✓		✓	✓		
gehorchen		✓	✓				✓

Infinitive	Trans.	Intrans.	Haben	Sein	Verb of Motion	Radical Change	Dative Verb
gehören		✓	✓				✓
gelingen		✓		✓			
geschehen		✓		✓		✓	
glauben	✓	✓	✓				
haben	✓		✓				
halten	✓		✓				
helfen		✓	✓				✓
kommen		✓		✓	✓		
lassen	✓		✓				
laufen		✓		✓	✓		
leben	✓		✓				
legen	✓		✓				
lesen	✓		✓				
liegen		✓	✓				
machen	✓		✓				
mitkommen		✓		✓	✓		
nehmen	✓		✓				
passieren		✓		✓		✓	
rennen		✓		✓	✓		
rufen	✓		✓				
schaden		✓		✓			✓
schlafen	✓		✓				
schlagen	✓		✓				
schliessen	✓		✓				
schreiben	✓		✓				
schwimmen		✓		✓	✓		
sehen	✓		✓				
sein		✓		✓		✓	
setzen	✓		✓				
singen	✓		✓				
sitzen		✓	✓				
sprechen	✓		✓				
springen		✓		✓	✓		
stehlen	✓		✓				
sterben		✓		✓		✓	

Infinitive	Trans.	Intrans.	Haben	Sein	Verb of Motion	Radical Change	Dative Verb
tragen	✓		✓				
treffen	✓		✓				
treten		✓		✓	✓		
trinken	✓		✓				
tun	✓		✓				
vergessen	✓		✓				
verlieren	✓		✓				
versprechen	✓		✓				✓
verstehen	✓		✓				
wachsen		✓		✓		✓	
warten		✓	✓				
waschen	✓		✓				
weinen	✓		✓				
werden		✓		✓		✓	
werfen	✓		✓				
wissen	✓		✓				
ziehen	✓		✓				
zusehen	✓		✓				✓

Conjunctions

Subordinating conjunctions require the conjugated verb to be the last element in the subordinate clause. The only exception occurs with double infinitive structures, which place the conjugated verb just before the double infinitive. Coordinate conjunctions do not require a change in word order.

Conjunction	Meaning	Verb at End of Clause	No Change
aber	but		✓
als	when, as	✓	
als ob	as if	✓	
als wenn	as if	✓	

Conjunction	Meaning	Verb at End of Clause	No Change
bevor	before	✓	
bis	until, up to	✓	
da	since	✓	
damit	so that	✓	
denn	because		✓
ehe	before	✓	
falls	in case	✓	
indem	during the time, while	✓	
nachdem	after	✓	
ob	whether	✓	
obwohl	although	✓	
oder	or		✓
seit	since	✓	
seitdem	since	✓	
so dass	so that	✓	
so . . . wie	as . . . as	✓	
sobald	as soon as	✓	
solange	as long as	✓	
sooft	as often as	✓	
soviel	as much as	✓	
soweit	as far as	✓	
und	and		✓
während	during	✓	
weil	because	✓	
wenn	whenever, if	✓	

Commonly Used Dative Verbs

Some dative verbs are verbs of motion and require *sein* as their auxiliary. Other dative verbs require *haben* as their auxiliary.

Infinitive	Meaning	Sein	Haben
antworten	to answer		✓
befehlen	to command		✓
begegnen	to encounter	✓	
danken	to thank		✓
dienen	to serve		✓
drohen	to threaten		✓
entkommen	to escape	✓	
entlaufen	to run away	✓	
erzählen	to narrate		✓
fehlen	to lack		✓
folgen	to follow	✓	
gehorchen	to obey		✓
gehören	to belong		✓
glauben	to believe		✓
gleichen	to equal		✓
gratulieren	to congratulate		✓
helfen	to help		✓
imponieren	to impress		✓
sich nähern	to approach		✓
nutzen (nützen)	to be of use		✓
raten	to advise		✓
sagen	to say		✓
schaden	to harm		✓
vertrauen	to trust		✓
zuhören	to listen to		✓
zusehen	to watch		✓
zustimmen	to agree		✓

Separable Prefixes and Their English Meanings

The separable prefixes separate from the stem of the verb in all tenses but the future. In the present and past tenses, the prefix is the last element in the sentence or clause. In the perfect tenses, the prefix is separated from the participle by the prefix *ge-*.

The prefix meaning given below is the general meaning, and other variations can occur. Notice that some of the separable prefixes can also be used as inseparable prefixes.

Prefix	*Approximate Meaning*	*Sep.*	*Insep.*
ab	away, off, of, departure	✓	
an	at, on, arrival	✓	
auf	up, open	✓	
aus	out of, finish	✓	
durch	through	✓	✓
ein	in	✓	
entgegen	toward	✓	
fort	away, departure	✓	
her	here	✓	
hin	away, down	✓	
hinter	behind, after	✓	✓
los	off, starting	✓	
mit	along	✓	
nach	after	✓	
über	over, extreme	✓	✓
um	around, turning, change	✓	✓
unter	under	✓	✓
voll	complete	✓	✓
vor	forward	✓	
weg	away	✓	
wider	against, contrary to	✓	✓
wieder	again, return	✓	✓
zu	to, close	✓	
zurück	back	✓	
zusammen	together	✓	

The following list of verbs with separable prefixes is a single example of each prefix. Numerous other verbs can use these prefixes, and the meanings derived by their use can go beyond what is presented here. These examples are only the generalization of the prefix meaning in its clearest form. For complete accuracy, you should look up verbs with a separable prefix in a dictionary.

abführen	to lead away
ansehen	to look at
aufmachen	to open
austrinken	to finish drinking
einsteigen	to get in, get on board
entgegenlaufen	to run toward
fortfahren	to drive away
herstellen	to place here
hinlegen	to lie down
losreißen	to pull off, tear off
mitkommen	to come along
nachstreben	to strive after
vorschreiten	to step forward, march on
weglaufen	to run away
zumachen	to close
zurücknehmen	to take back
zusammenbringen	to bring together

When the stress is on the stem of the verb, the prefix is used as an inseparable prefix. Take note of these examples:

*durch**dring**en*	to penetrate
*durch**web**en*	to interweave
*hinter**bleib**en*	to remain behind
*hinter**lass**en*	to leave behind
*über**rasch**en*	to surprise
*über**setz**en*	to translate
*um**arm**en*	to embrace
*um**bau**en*	to build around
*unter**brech**en*	to interrupt

*unter**drück**en*	to suppress
*voll**end**en*	to complete
*voll**zieh**en*	to carry out
*wider**sprech**en*	to contradict
*wider**steh**en*	to resist
*wieder**hol**en*	to repeat

The Verb *Get* in German

The English verb *get* has numerous uses. Depending upon the kind of phrase *get* is used in, it can derive a wide variety of meanings. Below is a list of uses of the verb and their German equivalents. Note that the verb **werden** is frequently a translation for *get* but not exclusively.

Get *with Adjectives or Participles*	*German Equivalent*
get acquainted	*kennenlernen*
get better	*besser werden*
get changed	*sich umziehen*
get cold	*kalt werden*
get dark	*dunkel werden*
get dressed	*sich anziehen*
get drunk	*sich betrinken*
get fat	*dick werden*
get hot	*heiß werden*
get hungry	*Hunger haben*
get hurt	*verletzt werden*
get lost	*verlorengehen*
get noisy	*laut werden*
get ready	*sich vorbereiten*
get thirsty	*Durst haben*
get undressed	*sich ausziehen*
get worse	*schlechter werden*

Get *with a Preposition*	*German Equivalent*
get along with	*auskommen mit*
get down	*heruntersteigen*
get from	*kommen aus, von*

Get *with a Preposition*	*German Equivalent*
get into	*eintreten*
get into (vehicles)	*einsteigen*
get off (vehicles)	*aussteigen*
get out of	*austreten*
get out of (vehicles)	*aussteigen*
get to	*kommen zu, in*
get up	*aufstehen*
get meaning *receive*	*bekommen, enthalten*
get something done	*lassen* + infinitive

Verbs of Obligation

Certain auxiliaries tell to what degree of obligation an action is performed. Some show great obligation; others show little obligation or willingness to perform an action.

English Auxiliary	*Degree of Obligation*	*German Auxiliary*
have to	greatest obligation	*müssen*
must	greatest obligation	*müssen*
should	great obligation	*sollen*
be supposed to	great obligation	*sollen*
ought to	some obligation	*sollen*
need to	little obligation	*brauchen*
can	capable but not obliged	*können*
be able to	capable but not obliged	*können*
may	permitted but not obliged	*dürfen*
want to	willing but not obliged	*wollen*
would like to	very willing but not obliged	*möchten* (plural subjunctive II)

Appendix A: Irregular Verbs and Their Principal Parts

In the present tense, the second-person singular and third-person singular are illustrated. In the past tense, the third person singular is illustrated. In the present tense of *sein* and *tun*, all persons are illustrated.

Infinitive	Present	Past	Past Participle	Past Subjunctive
backen	bäckst bäckt	buk or backte	gebacken	büke or backte
befehlen	befiehlst befiehlt	befahl	befohlen	beföhle
befleißen	befleißt befleißt	befliss	beflissen	beflisse
beginnen	beginnst beginnt	begann	begonnen	begönne
beißen	beißt beißt	biss	gebissen	bisse
bergen	birgst birgt	barg	geborgen	bürge
bersten	birst birst	barst	geborsten	börste

Infinitive	*Present*	*Past*	*Past Participle*	*Past Subjunctive*
betrügen	betrügst betrügt	betrog	betrogen	betröge
bewegen	bewegst bewegt	bewog	bewogen	bewöge
biegen	biegst biegt	bog	gebogen	böge
bieten	bietest bietet	bot	geboten	böte
binden	bindest bindet	band	gebunden	bände
bitten	bittest bittet	bat	gebeten	bäte
blasen	bläst bläst	blies	geblasen	bliese
bleiben	bleibst bleibt	blieb	geblieben	bliebe
bleichen	bleichst bleicht	blich	geblichen	bliche
braten	brätst brät	briet	gebraten	briete
brechen	brichst bricht	brach	gebrochen	bräche
brennen	brennst brennt	brannte	gebrannt	brennte
bringen	bringst bringt	brachte	gebracht	brächte
denken	denkst denkt	dachte	gedacht	dächte
dingen	dingst dingt	dingte or dang	gedungen or gedingt	dingte
dreschen	drischst drischt	drasch	gedroschen	drösche
dringen	dringst dringt	drang	gedrungen	dränge

Infinitive	Present	Past	Past Participle	Past Subjunctive
dürfen	darfst darf	durfte	gedürft	dürfte
empfangen	empfängst empfängt	empfing	empfangen	empfinge
empfehlen	empfiehlst empfiehlt	empfahl	empfohlen	empföhle
empfinden	empfindest empfindet	empfand	empfunden	empfände
erbleichen	erbleichst erbleicht	erbleichte or erblich	erbleicht or erblichen	erbleichte or erbliche
erlöschen	erlischst erlischt	erlosch	erloschen	erlösche
erschrecken	erschrickst erschrickt	erschrak	erschrocken	erschräke
erwägen	erwägst erwägt	erwog	erwogen	erwöge
essen	isst isst	aß	gegessen	ässe
fahren	fährst fährt	fuhr	gefahren	führe
fallen	fällst fällt	fiel	gefallen	fiele
fangen	fängst fängt	fing	gefangen	finge
fechten	fichtest ficht	focht	gefochten	föchte
finden	findest findet	fand	gefunden	fände
flechten	flichtest flicht	flocht	geflochten	flöchte
fliegen	fliegst fliegt	flog	geflogen	flöge
fliehen	fliehst flieht	floh	geflohen	flöhe

Infinitive	Present	Past	Past Participle	Past Subjunctive
fließen	fließt fließt	floss	geflossen	flösse
fressen	frisst frisst	fraß	gefressen	frässe
frieren	frierst friert	fror	gefroren	fröre
gären	gärst gärt	gor	gegoren	göre
gebären	gebierst gebiert	gebar	geboren	gebäre
geben	gibst gibt	gab	gegeben	gäbe
gedeihen	gedeihst gedeiht	gedieh	gediehen	gediehe
gehen	gehst geht	ging	gegangen	ginge
gelten	giltst gilt	galt	gegolten	gälte or gölte
genesen	genest genest	genas	genesen	genäse
genießen	genießt genießt	genoss	genossen	genösse
geraten	gerätst gerät	geriet	geraten	geriete
gewinnen	gewinnst gewinnt	gewann	gewonnen	gewänne or gewönne
gießen	gießt gießt	goss	gegossen	gösse
gleichen	gleichst gleicht	glich	geglichen	gliche
gleiten	gleitest gleitet	glitt	geglitten	glitte
glimmen	glimmst glimmt	glomm or glimmte	geglommen or geglimmt	glömme or glimmte

Infinitive	Present	Past	Past Participle	Past Subjunctive
graben	gräbst gräbt	grub	gegraben	grübe
greifen	greifst greift	griff	gegriffen	griffe
haben	hast hat	hatte	gehabt	hätte
halten	hältst hält	hielt	gehalten	hielte
hangen	hängst hängt	hing	gehangen	hinge
hauen	haust haut	hieb	gehauen	hiebe
heben	hebst hebt	hob	gehoben	höbe
heißen	heißt heißt	hieß	geheißen	hieße
helfen	hilfst hilft	half	geholfen	hülfe
kennen	kennst kennt	kannte	gekannt	kennte
klimmen	klimmst klimmt	klomm or klimmte	geklommen or geklimmt	klömme or klimmte
klingen	klingst klingt	klang	geklungen	klänge
kneifen	kneifst kneift	kniff	gekniffen	kniffe
kommen	kommst kommt	kam	gekommen	käme
können	kannst kann	konnte	gekonnt	könnte
kriechen	kriechst kriecht	kroch	gekrochen	kröche
laden	lädst or ladest lädt or ladet	lud or ladete	geladen or geladet	lüde or ladete

Infinitive	Present	Past	Past Participle	Past Subjunctive
lassen	lässt lässt	ließ	gelassen	ließe
laufen	läufst läuft	lief	gelaufen	liefe
leiden	leidest leidet	litt	gelitten	litte
leihen	leihst leiht	lieh	geliehen	liehe
lesen	liest liest	las	gelesen	läse
liegen	liegst liegt	lag	gelegen	läge
lügen	lügst lügt	log	gelogen	löge
mahlen	mahlst mahlt	mahlte	gemahlen	mahlte
meiden	meidest meidet	mied	gemieden	miede
melken	melkst melkt	melkte	gemelkt or gemolken (adjective)	mölke
messen	misst misst	maß	gemessen	mässe
mögen	magst mag	mochte	gemocht	möchte
müssen	musst muss	musste	gemusst	müsste
nehmen	nimmst nimmt	nahm	genommen	nähme
nennen	nennst nennt	nannte	genannt	nennte
pfeifen	pfeifst pfeift	pfiff	gepfiffen	pfiffe

Infinitive	Present	Past	Past Participle	Past Subjunctive
pflegen	pflegst pflegt	pflegte or pflog	gepflegt or gepflogen	pflegte or pflöge
preisen	preist preist	pries	gepriesen	priese
quellen	quillst quillt	quoll	gequollen	quölle
raten	rätst rät	riet	geraten	riete
reiben	reibst reibt	rieb	gerieben	riebe
reißen	reißt reißt	riss	gerissen	risse
reiten	reitest reitet	ritt	geritten	ritte
rennen	rennst rennt	rannte	gerannt	rennte
riechen	riechst riecht	roch	gerochen	röche
ringen	ringst ringt	rang	gerungen	ränge
rinnen	rinnst rinnt	rann	geronnen	rönne
rufen	rufst ruft	rief	gerufen	riefe
salzen	salzt salzt	salzte	gesalzt or gesalzen (figurative)	salzte
saufen	säufst säuft	soff	gesoffen	söffe
saugen	saugst saugt	sog	gesogen	söge
schaffen	schaffst schafft	schuf	geschaffen	schüfe

Infinitive	*Present*	*Past*	*Past Participle*	*Past Subjunctive*
schallen	schallst schallt	schallte	geschallt	schallte or schölle
scheiden	scheidest scheidet	schied	geschieden	schiede
scheinen	scheinst scheint	schien	geschienen	schiene
schelten	schiltst schilt	schalt	gescholten	schölte
scheren	schierst schiert	schor or scherte	geschoren or geschert	schöre or scherte
schieben	schiebst schiebt	schob	geschoben	schöbe
schießen	schießt schießt	schoss	geschossen	schösse
schinden	schindest schindet	schund	geschunden	schünde
schlafen	schläfst schläft	schlief	geschlafen	schliefe
schlagen	schlägst schlägt	schlug	geschlagen	schlüge
schleichen	schleichst schleicht	schlich	geschlichen	schliche
schleifen	schleifst schleift	schliff	geschliffen	schliffe
schleißen	schleißt schleißt	schliss	geschlissen	schlisse
schliefen	schliefst schlieft	schloff	geschloffen	schlöffe
schließen	schließt schließt	schloss	geschlossen	schlösse
schlingen	schlingst schlingt	schlang	geschlungen	schlänge
schmeißen	schmeißt schmeißt	schmiss	geschmissen	schmisse

Infinitive	Present	Past	Past Participle	Past Subjunctive
schmelzen	schmilzt schmilzt	schmolz	geschmolzen	schmölze
schneiden	schneidest schneidet	schnitt	geschnitten	schnitte
schrecken	schrickst schrickt	schrak	geschrocken	schräke
schreiben	schreibst schreibt	schrieb	geschrieben	schriebe
schreien	schreist schreit	schrie	geschrieen	schriee
schreiten	schreitest schreitet	schritt	geschritten	schritte
schweigen	schweigst schweigt	schwieg	geschwiegen	schwiege
schwellen	schwillst schwillt	schwoll	geschwollen	schwölle
schwimmen	schwimmst schwimmt	schwamm	geschwommen	schwömme
schwinden	schwindest schwindet	schwand	geschwunden	schwände
schwingen	schwingst schwingt	schwang	geschwungen	schwänge
schwören	schwörst schwört	schwur	geschworen	schwüre
sehen	siehst sieht	sah	gesehen	sähe
sein	bin bist ist sind seid sind	war	gewesen	wäre
senden	sendest sendet	sandte or sendete	gesandt or gesendet	sendete
sieden	siedest siedet	sott or siedete	gesotten	sötte or siedete
singen	singst singt	sang	gesungen	sänge

Infinitive	*Present*	*Past*	*Past Participle*	*Past Subjunctive*
sinken	sinkst sinkt	sank	gesunken	sänke
sinnen	sinnst sinnt	sann	gesonnen	sänne
sitzen	sitzt sitzt	saß	gesessen	sässe
sollen	sollst soll	sollte	gesollt	sollte
spalten	spaltest spaltet	spaltete	gespalten or gespaltet	spaltete
speien	speist speit	spie	gespieen	spiee
spinnen	spinnst spinnt	spann	gesponnen	spönne
spleißen	spleißt spleißt	spliss	gesplissen	splisse
sprechen	sprichst spricht	sprach	gesprochen	spräche
sprießen	sprießt sprießt	spross	gesprossen	sprösse
springen	springst springt	sprang	gesprungen	spränge
stechen	stichst sticht	stach	gestochen	stäche
stecken	steckst steckt	steckte or stak	gesteckt	steckte or stäke
stehen	stehst steht	stand	gestanden	stünde or stände
stehlen	stiehlst stiehlt	stahl	gestohlen	stöhle
steigen	steigst steigt	stieg	gestiegen	stiege
sterben	stirbst stirbt	starb	gestorben	stürbe

Infinitive	Present	Past	Past Participle	Past Subjunctive
stieben	stiebst	stob or	gestoben or	stöbe or
	stiebt	stiebte	gestiebt	stiebte
stinken	stinkst	stank	gestunken	stänke
	stinkt			
stoßen	stößt	stieß	gestoßen	stieße
	stößt			
streichen	streichst	strich	gestrichen	striche
	streicht			
streiten	streitest	stritt	gestritten	stritte
	streitet			
tragen	trägst	trug	getragen	trüge
	trägt			
treffen	triffst	traf	getroffen	träfe
	trifft			
treiben	treibst	trieb	getrieben	triebe
	treibt			
treten	trittst	trat	getreten	träte
	tritt			
triefen	triefst	troff	getrieft	tröffe
	trieft			
trinken	trinkst	trank	getrunken	tränke
	trinkt			
tun	tue tust tut	tat	getan	täte
	tun tut tun			
verderben	verdirbst	verdarb	verdorben	verdürbe
	verdirbt			
verdrießen	verdrießt	verdross	verdrossen	verdrösse
vergessen	vergisst	vergaß	vergessen	vergässe
	vergisst			
verhehlen	verhehlst	verhelte	verhehlt or	verhelte
	verhehlt		verhohlen	
verlieren	verlierst	verlor	verloren	verlöre
	verliert			

Infinitive	Present	Past	Past Participle	Past Subjunctive
verwirren	verwirrst verwirrt	verwirrte	verwirrt or verworren (adjective)	verwirrte
wachsen	wächst wächst	wuchs	gewachsen	wüchse
wägen	wägst wägt	wog or wägte	gewogen	wöge or wägte
waschen	wäschst wäscht	wusch	gewaschen	wüsche
weichen	weichst weicht	wich	gewichen	wiche
weisen	weist weist	wies	gewiesen	wiese
wenden	wendest wendet	wandte or wendete	gewandt or gewendet	wendete
werben	wirbst wirbt	warb	geworben	würbe
werden	wirst wird	wurde	geworden	würde
werfen	wirfst wirft	warf	geworfen	würfe
wiegen	wiegst wiegt	wog	gewogen	wöge
winden	windest windet	wand	gewunden	wände
wissen	weißt weiß	wusste	gewusst	wüsste
wollen	willst will	wollte	gewollt	wollte
zeihen	zeihst zeiht	zieh	geziehen	ziehe
ziehen	ziehst zieht	zog	gezogen	zöge
zwingen	zwingst zwingt	zwang	gezwungen	zwänge

Some irregular verbs are used in impersonal expressions and are conjugated only with the third person.

Infinitive	Present	Past	Past Participle	Past Subjunctive
dünken	dünkt deucht	deuchte or dünkte	gedeucht or gedünkt	deuchte or dünkte
gelingen	gelingt	gelang	gelungen	gelänge
geschehen	geschieht	geschah	geschehen	geschähe
misslingen	misslingt	misslang	misslungen	misslänge
schwären	schwärt or schwiert	schwor	geschworen	schwöre
verschallen	verschillt	verscholl	verschollen	verschölle

Appendix B:
Verbs and Prepositions

This appendix offers a variety of high-frequency verbs and the prepositions that usually accompany them. Each infinitive is followed by an example sentence in German and its English translation.

Verbs that Require the Accusative Case
achten **auf**
Ich achte sehr darauf, niemanden zu verletzen.
I'm careful not to hurt anybody.

sich anlehnen **an**
Der faule Junge lehnt sich mit dem Rücken **an die** Tür.
The lazy boy leans his back against the door.

antworten **auf**
Er antwortet dem Dozenten **auf** die Fragen.
He answered the lecturer's questions.

sich ärgern **über**
Ärgere dich nicht dar**über**!
Don't let yourself get upset by it!

aufpassen **auf**
Ich muss **auf** meinen Bruder aufpassen.
I have to look after my brother.

aufschreiben **gegen**
Der Arzt schreibt mir etwas **gegen** Bauchschmerzen auf.
The doctor prescribes something for my stomach pains.

sich beklagen **über**
Martin beklagte sich **über** die kalte Suppe.
Martin complained about the cold soup.

beneiden **um**
Karl beneidet mich **um** meine Stelle.
Karl envies me for my job.

berichten **über**
Der Reporter hat etwas Neues **über** den Krieg zu berichten.
The reporter has something new to report about the war.

sich beschweren **über**
Eine ältere Dame beschwert sich **über** den kalten Tee.
An elderly woman complains about the cold tea.

sich beteiligen **an**
Alle haben sich **an** seinem Geburtstagsgeschenk beteiligt.
Everyone chipped in for his birthday present.

sich bewerben **um**
Der Reisende hat sich **um** ein Visum beworben.
The traveler applied for a visa.

bezahlen **für**
Haben Sie **für** das Essen bezahlt?
Did you pay for the meal?

sich beziehen **auf**
Worauf beziehen Sie sich?
What are you referring to?

bitten **um**
Darf ich **um** Ihren Namen bitten?
May I ask for your name?

blicken **auf**
Die Touristen blicken **auf** den schönen See.
The tourists look out at the beautiful lake.

danken **für**
Ich danke euch **für** das Geschenk.
Thanks to all of you for the gift.

denken **an**
Ich denke oft **an** Oma.
I often think about granny.

diskutieren **über**
Worüber diskutiert ihr?
What is your discussion about?

sich drehen **um**
Das Gespräch drehte sich **um** die wirtschaftliche Lage.
The conversation revolved around the economic situation.

drücken **auf**
Drücken Sie bitte **auf** die oberste Taste.
Please press the uppermost key.

sich einmischen **in**
Warum willst du dich **in** meine Angelegenheiten einmischen?
Why do you want to interfere in my affairs?

einweisen **in**
Doktor Schmidt hat sie **in** diese Klinik eingewiesen.
Dr. Schmidt sent her to this clinic.

entscheiden **über**
Der Arzt muss **über** die Operation entscheiden.
The physician has to decide about the operation.

sich erinnern **an**
Sie erinnerte mich dar**an**, dass wir morgen nach Paris fahren.
She reminded me that we're going to Paris tomorrow.

ersetzen **durch**
Dieser Computer hat sich leicht **durch** einen anderen ersetzen lassen.
This computer was easily replaced by another one.

erzählen **über**
Erzähle uns bitte etwas **über** deine Afrikareise!
Please tell us something about your trip to Africa!

fließen **durch**
Welcher Fluss fließt **durch** Berlin?
What river flows through Berlin?

sich freuen **auf**
Die Schüler freuen sich schon **auf** die Ferien.
The pupils are already looking forward to vacation.

sich freuen **über**
Ich habe mich **über** deinen letzten Brief gefreut.
I was very pleased with your last letter.

gehen **um**
Wie immer ging es **um** das Geld.
As usual it had to do with money.

sich gewöhnen **an**
Er hat sich noch nicht **an** die Großstadt gewöhnt.
He still hasn't gotten used to the big city.

glauben **an**
Glauben Sie **an** Gott?
Do you believe in God?

sich handeln **um**
Es handelt sich **um** Geld.
It's a matter of money.

hängen **an**
Ich hänge das Bild **an** die Wand.
I'll hang the picture on the wall.

hängen **über**
Wer hängte dieses Bild **über** das Bett?
Who hung this picture over the bed?

impfen **gegen**
Sie haben das Kind **gegen** Grippe geimpft.
They inoculated the child against influenza.

sich informieren **über**
Sie versuchen sich **über** diese neuen Gefahren zu informieren.
They try to inform themselves about these new dangers.

sich interessieren **für**
Mein Sohn interessiert sich **für** alle Wissenschaften.
My son is interested in all sciences.

kämpfen **für**
Sie kämpfen **für** bessere Umweltschutzgesetze.
They're fighting for better protective, environmental laws.

kämpfen **gegen**
Die Soldaten kämpfen **gegen** den Feind.
The soldiers fight against the enemy.

klagen **gegen**
Sie hat vor Gericht **gegen** ihre Nachbarn geklagt.
She sued her neighbors in court.

sich kümmern **um**
Herr Schneider hat sich **um** seine Frau gekümmert.
Mr. Schneider took care of his wife.

lachen **über**
Alle lachen **über** seinen komischen Witz.
Everyone is laughing at his funny joke.

sich mischen **unter**
Die Gastgeberin mischt sich **unter** die Gäste.
The hostess is mingling among her guests.

nachdenken **über**
Haben Sie schon **über** mein Problem nachgedacht?
Did you already give my problem some thought?

protestieren **gegen**
Viele Studenten haben **gegen** den Krieg protestiert.
Many students protested against the war.

reden **über**
Wir reden gerade **über** seine neue Theorie.
Right now we're talking about his new theory.

schieben **an**
Er will den Schrank **an** die Wand schieben.
He wants to shove the cabinet against the wall.

schimpfen **über**
Viele Leute schimpfen **über** den Bürgermeister.
Many people are complaining about the mayor.

schreiben **in**
Sie schreibt etwas **in** ihr Heft.
She's writing something in her notebook.

sein **gegen**
Vater ist da**gegen**, wieder ans Mittelmeer zu fahren.
Father is against going to the Mediterranean again.

sein verliebt **in**
Sie ist nicht mehr **in** ihn verliebt.
She's not in love with him anymore.

sein **von**
Das ist ein Geschenk **von** Tante Luise.
That's a gift from Aunt Luise.

sorgen **für**
Wer kann **für** den alten Herrn sorgen?
Who is able to look after the old gentleman?

sparen **auf**
Mein jüngster Bruder spart **auf** ein neues Auto.
My youngest brother is saving for a new car.

sprechen **über**
Ich möchte heute **über** ein neues Problem sprechen.
Today I'd like to speak about a new problem.

stecken **in**
Sie steckt das Geld **in** eine Tasche.
She puts the money in a pocket.

stellen **an**
Sie stellte die neue Vase **an** die Wand.
She placed the new vase against the wall.

stellen **auf**
Wer hat den Eimer **auf** den Esstisch gestellt?
Who put the pail on the dining room table?

steigen **um**
Neulich sind die Preise **um** fünfzehn Prozent gestiegen.
Prices recently rose by fifteen percent.

streiten **über**
Sie haben immer **über** Politik gestritten.
They've always argued about politics.

sich stützen **auf**
Ich stütze mich mit beiden Händen **auf** den Schreibtisch.
I support myself on the desk with both hands.

sich unterhalten **über**
Sie unterhalten sich **über** die politische Entwicklung in Europa.
They're talking about the political development in Europe.

sich verlassen **auf**
Sie können sich **auf** mich verlassen.
You can rely on me.

sich verlieben **in**
Martin hat sich **in** eine hübsche Französin verliebt.
Martin fell in love with a beautiful French girl.

verzichten **auf**
Man muss **auf** vieles verzichten, wenn man arm ist.
You have to give up a lot when you're poor.

warten **auf**
Wir haben lange **auf** dich gewartet.
We waited for you for a long time.

sich wenden **an**
Ich habe mich **an** das Postamt gewandt.
I contacted the post office.

sich wehren **gegen**
Wer kann sich da**gegen** wehren?
Who can protect himself from it?

weinen **über**
Wor**über** weint er so?
What's he crying about like that?

ziehen **an**
Sie zieht einen Hocker **an** den Tisch.
She pulls a stool up to the table.

Verbs That Require the Dative Case
abhangen **von**
Es hängt **von** dir ab.
It depends upon you.

abholen **von**
Sie hat ihn **vom** Bahnhof abgeholt.
She picked him up from the train station.

aufbewahren **in**
Er bewahrt seine Ringe **im** Schrank auf.
He stores away his rings in the wardrobe.

auskommen **mit**
Wir werden da**mit** auskommen.
We'll get by with it.

ausstatten **mit**
Das neue Haus wird **mit** allem Komfort ausgestattet werden.
The new house will be equipped with every comfort.

sich bedanken **bei**
Ich möchte mich **bei** Ihnen bedanken.
I'd like to thank you.

befreien **von**
Der reiche Mann hat uns **von** unseren finanziellen Sorgen befreit.
The rich man freed us from our financial worries.

beitragen **zu**
Alle haben **zum** Fest beigetragen.
Everyone contributed to the party.

sich beklagen **bei**
Sie hat sich **bei** ihrem Rechtsanwalt beklagt.
She made a complaint to her lawyer.

bekommen **von**
Von wem hast du es bekommen?
From whom did you get it?

sich beschäftigen **mit**
Er beschäftigt sich **mit** dem neuen Computer.
He's busy with the new computer.

beschützen **vor**
Wer wird uns **vor** unseren Feinden beschützen?
Who will protect us from our enemies?

bestehen **aus**
Dieses Werk besteht **aus** fünf Bänden.
This work consists of five volumes.

bestimmen **zu**
Wir sind alle da**zu** bestimmt.
We are all destined for that.

bestrafen **mit**
Der Richter wollte den Einbrecher **mit** Gefängnis bestrafen.
The judge wanted to punish the burglar with a prison sentence.

bleiben **bei**
Der Rechtsanwalt ist **bei** seiner Aussage geblieben.
The lawyer remained with his original statement.

dienen **bei**
Die junge Frau dient jetzt **bei** einer reichen Dame.
The young woman is now in service in the home of a rich lady.

drohen **mit**
Der Fremde drohte ihr **mit** einem Messer.
The stranger threatened her with a knife.

eignen **zu**
Der junge Mann ist leider nicht da**zu** geeignet.
The young man is unfortunately not qualified for it.

sich entschuldigen **bei**
Er musste sich **bei** seiner beleidigten Tante entschuldigen.
He had to apologize to his offended aunt.

sich erholen **von**
Großmutter hat sich **von** der Krankheit gut erholt.
Grandmother recovered well from the illness.

sich erkälten **bei**
Karl hat sich **beim** Schwimmen erkältet.
Karl caught a cold while swimming.

erkennen **an**
Ich erkenne ihn **an** der Stimme.
I recognize him by his voice.

sich erkundigen **nach**
Ich habe mich **nach** billigen Flügen nach Europa erkundigt.
I inquired about cheap flights to Europe.

sich ernähren **von**
Der Sportler ernährt sich nur **von** Fleisch und Früchten.
The athlete eats only meat and fruit.

erwarten **von**
Ich erwarte **von** euch, dass ihr euch besser benehmt.
I expect you to behave yourselves better.

erzählen **von**
Frau Kamps hat **von** ihrer Spanienreise erzählt.
Mrs. Kamps told about her trip to Spain.

fahren **mit** (transport)
Ich fahre lieber **mit** dem Zug.
I prefer traveling by train.

sich festhalten **an**
Sie hält sich mit beiden Händen **an** ihrem Mann fest.
She holds onto her husband with both hands.

fliehen **vor**
Die Bevölkerung flieht **vor** dem Feind.
The population flees from the enemy.

fragen **nach**
Hat jemand **nach** uns gefragt?
Did anyone ask about us?

gehören **zu**
Angelika gehört **zu** einem Sportverein.
Angelika belongs to a sports club.

hängen **an**
Das Bild hängt **an** der Wand.
The picture is hanging on the wall.

hängen **über**
Was für ein Bild hängt **über** dem Bett?
What kind of picture is hanging over the bed?

herauskommen **aus**
Er hat den Bären **aus** der Waldhütte herauskommen sehen.
He saw the bear coming out of the cabin.

holen **aus**
Ich hole ein paar Flaschen Bier **aus** dem Keller.
I get a couple bottles of beer from the cellar.

sich hüten **vor**
Man muss sich **vor** Taschendieben hüten.
You have to guard against pickpockets.

importieren **aus**
Japan importiert Weizen **aus** den USA.
Japan imports wheat from the USA.

kommen **aus**
Mein Onkel kommt **aus** Hannover.
My uncle comes from Hanover.

lesen **aus**
Was lesen Sie **aus** diesem Briefe?
What is your understanding of this letter?

lesen **in**
Ich habe etwas Interessantes **in** diesem Buch gelesen.
I read something interesting in this book.

sich melden **bei**
Er wird sich **bei** uns melden, wenn er wieder in Bremen ist.
He'll get in touch with us when he's in Bremen again.

operieren **an**
Meine Tante muss **am** Herz operiert werden.
My aunt has to have heart surgery.

reisen **in**
Im Januar reisen wir **in** den Süden.
In January we're traveling to the south.

reisen **nach**
Warum will Vater **nach** Italien reisen?
Why does father want to travel to Italy?

riechen **nach**
In der Küche riecht es **nach** Kohl.
It smells of cabbage in the kitchen.

schlafen **mit**
Sie schlafen **mit**einander.
They sleep with one another.

schmecken **nach**
Meine Suppe schmeckt **nach** Seife!
My soup tastes like soap!

schützen **vor**
Sie versuchte ihren Sohn **vor** schlechten Einflüssen zu schützen.
She tried to protect her son from bad influences.

sich sehnen **nach**
Ich sehne mich so **nach** meinen Eltern.
I miss my parents so much.

sein **aus** (from)
Sind Ihre Eltern **aus** Italien?
Are your parents from Italy?

sein **aus** (made of)
Seine neue Armbanduhr ist **aus** Gold.
His new watch is made of gold.

sein einverstanden **mit**
Sind Sie **mit** dem Vertrag einverstanden?
Are you in agreement with the contract?

sprechen **von**
Wir werden noch da**von** sprechen müssen.
We're still going to have to talk about it.

springen **in**
Plötzlich springen die Kinder **ins** Wasser.
Suddenly the children jump into the water.

springen **über**
Der kleine Hund kann **über** den Zaun springen.
The little dog can jump over the fence.

stechen **mit**
Er hat sich **mit** der Nadel in die Hand gestochen.
He pricked his hand with the needle.

stehen **an**
Jemand steht **am** Fenster.
Someone is standing at the window.

stehen **auf**
Eine kleine Vase stand **auf** dem Schreibtisch.
A little vase stood on the desk.

sterben **an**
Onkel Heinz ist **an** Krebs gestorben.
Uncle Heinz died from cancer.

stinken **nach**
Hier stinkt es **nach** Benzin.
It smells of gasoline here.

suchen **nach**
Die Katze sucht in allen Ecken **nach** der Maus.
The cat is looking in every corner for the mouse.

tasten **nach**
Ich taste im dunklen Zimmer **nach** der Lampe.
I feel around in the dark room for the lamp.

teilnehmen **an**
Darf ein Kind **an** einem Schachspiel teilnehmen?
Can a child participate in a chess game?

träumen **von**
Er träumt da**von**, Millionär zu werden.
He dreams of becoming a millionaire.

sich trennen **von**
Karl will sich nicht **von** seiner Frau trennen.
Karl doesn't want to separate from his wife.

überzeugen **von**
Ich bin da**von** überzeugt, dass die Preise steigen werden.
I'm convinced that prices will rise.

sich unterscheiden **von**
Sie unterscheidet sich **von** ihrer Schwester durch ihre blauen Augen.
Her blue eyes make her different from her sister.

sich verbrennen **an**
Der Junge hat sich **an** einer Zigarre verbrannt.
The boy burned himself on a cigar.

verlangen **von**
Der Manager verlangt **von** uns, an der Besprechung teilzunehmen.
The manager demands that we take part in the conference.

sich verletzen **bei**
Ingrid verletzt sich **beim** Fußballspielen.
Ingrid hurt herself playing soccer.

verstecken **in**
Ich verstecke das Geld **in** einer Höhle.
I hide the money in a cave.

verurteilen **zu**
Er wird den Taschendieb **zu** zwei Jahren Gefängnis verurteilen.
He'll sentence the pickpocket to two years in prison.

verwechseln **mit**
Ich habe Martin **mit** seinem Bruder verwechselt.
I mistook Martin for his brother.

weinen **vor**
Sie weinte **vor** Freude.
She cried from joy.

werden **aus**
Was soll **aus** ihm werden?
What is going to become of him?

wissen **von**
Seine Mutter wusste nichts da**von**.
His mother didn't know anything about it.

wohnen **bei**
Frau Krebs wird **bei** ihrer Schwester wohnen.
Mrs. Krebs is going to live at her sister's house.

ziehen **nach**
Seine Eltern werden **nach** Berlin ziehen.
His parents will move to Berlin.

zudecken **mit**
Sie deckte das Kind **mit** der Bettdecke gut zu.
She snugly covered the child with the blanket.

Answer Key

Chapter 1

Exercise 1
1. Der Amerikaner hat seinen deutschen Freund besucht.
2. Gestern hatte ich keine Zeit dazu.
3. Wir wissen, dass du es nicht hast lernen können.
4. Ich bin (war) nicht der Ansicht.
5. Das Bild ist von dem Maler gemalt worden.
6. Es wird (wurde) sehr heiß.
7. Die Wunden werden (wurden) von einem jungen Arzt geheilt.
8. Wen haben Sie gefragt?
9. Seid ihr den ausländischen Studenten begegnet?
10. Wenn das Buch nicht interessant wäre, würde er es nicht lesen.

Chapter 2

Exercise 1
1. Im Februar reisen wir mit Verwandten nach Spanien.
2. Nach dem Krieg kamen die Flüchtlinge langsam nach Hause.
3. Als Onkel Peter zu Besuch kam, kaufte Vater ein neues Bett.
4. Später ging Herr Doktor Schmidt zum Krankenhaus zurück.
5. Schnell lief der weinende Junge ins Wohnzimmer.

Exercise 2
1. Den ganzen Tag war Karl in der Stadt.
2. Schach spielen die Kinder.
3. Nächste Woche fahre ich in die Schweiz.

4. Als er in Hamburg war, besuchte er eine Freundin.

5. Morgen gehen wir wieder in die Schule.

Exercise 3

1. Wen hat die Polizei verhaftet?
   Wen hatte die Polizei verhaftet?

2. Am Abend ist Herr Schneider von der Arbeit nach Hause gekommen.
   Am Abend war Herr Schneider von der Arbeit nach Hause gekommen.

3. Als Klaudia in der Bäckerei gewesen ist, ist sie Herrn Kraus begegnet.
   Als Klaudia in der Bäckerei gewesen war, war sie Herrn Kraus begegnet.

Exercise 4

1. Die alten Leute wollen im Garten spazieren.

2. Ich musste bis in die Nacht arbeiten.

3. Frau Brenner kann ihre Meinung nicht rechtfertigen.

4. Sie hat ihre Hausarbeit tun sollen.

Exercise 5

1. Ich wusste nicht, dass er den Wecker hat reparieren lassen.

2. Ich wusste nicht, dass du mit dem letzten Zug gekommen bist.

3. Ich wusste nicht, dass die alte Dame den Dieb hat weglaufen sehen.

4. Ich wusste nicht, dass die Kinder großen Hunger gehabt haben.

5. Ich wusste nicht, dass sie einen neuen Computer hat kaufen wollen.

Exercise 6

Sample answers are given.

1. Meine Kusine wohnt in Tschechien, und mein Vetter wohnt in Ungarn.

2. Die Zwillinge sind zehn Jahre alt, aber mein ältester Sohn ist achtzehn.

3. Er hat sein Gepäck verloren, während er eine Reise nach Italien machte.
4. Franziska ist noch im Bett, weil sie sich erkältet hat.
5. Der Roman ist nicht interessant, sondern sehr langweilig.

Chapter 3

Exercise 1
1. Der Schüler hat dem Lehrer sofort geantwortet.
2. Die Mutter drohte dem kleinen Kind mit dem Finger.
3. Es scheint mir, dass du wieder krank bist.
4. Er dankte seiner Tante für das Geschenk.
5. Das Konzert hat ihm sehr imponiert.

Exercise 2
1. Der Alkohol hat dem Gehirn geschadet.
2. Ein gutes Wörterbuch hat einem Studenten nützen können.
3. Der lange Zug hat sich dem Hauptbahnhof genähert.
4. Die Hunde haben dem Herrn überall folgen wollen.
5. Der rote Apfel hat dem lächelnden Jungen sehr gut geschmeckt.

Exercise 3
1. Wir danken unseren neuen Freunden.
   Wir besuchen unsere neuen Freunde.
2. Der Kellner dient den unhöflichen Kunden.
   Der Kellner beschreibt die unhöflichen Kunden.
3. Ich imponiere meinem Professor.
   Ich enttäusche meinen Professor.
4. Der alte Hund folgt dem fremden Mann.
   Der alte Hund findet den fremden Mann.

Chapter 4

Exercise 1

1. Du hast dich angezogen.
2. Sie erinnert sich an ihren Hochzeitstag.
3. Wie könnt ihr euch ändern?
4. Ich frage mich, ob wir genug gespart haben.
5. Haben Sie sich wieder geärgert?

Exercise 2

Sample answers are given.

1. Sie haben sich geirrt.
2. Die Kinder waschen sich im Badezimmer.
3. Klaudia beeilt sich immer.
4. Die müden Soldaten ziehen sich langsam aus.
5. Ich frage mich, ob du wirklich Recht hast.

Chapter 5

Exercise 1

1. Klaudia möchte sich einen neuen Wagen kaufen.
2. Meine Schwestern haben sich die schönen Röcke angezogen.
3. Wo kann ich mir die Hände waschen?
4. Kannst du dir nicht verzeihen?
5. Dürfen wir uns ein Stück Kuchen nehmen?

Exercise 2

Sample answers are given.

1. Der Knabe zieht eine alte Jacke an.
2. Du musst die gelbe Bluse ausziehen.
3. Ich ziehe meine Schuhe um.

Exercise 3

Sample answers are given.

1. Sein Bruder will sich nicht anziehen.
2. Ich habe mich schon ausgezogen.
3. Müssen wir uns jetzt umziehen?

Exercise 4

Sample answers are given.

1. Die Kinder ziehen sich die warmen Handschuhe an.
2. Meine Mutter hat sich den langen Rock ausgezogen.
3. Ich ziehe mir die Stiefel um.

Exercise 5

1. Martin widerspricht sich.
2. Kannst du dir nicht verzeihen?
3. Tante Luise hat sich einen Pelzmantel gekauft.
4. Sie helfen sich, so gut Sie können.
5. Ich habe mir die Schuhe ausgezogen.
6. Kinder, habt ihr euch die Haare gekämmt?

Chapter 6

Exercise 1

1. Der Stoff ist mit Blumen durchwoben.
2. Wie können wir dir die Arbeit erleichtern?
3. Gestern bekam ich ein Geschenk von Oma.
4. Warum haben Sie Ihre Dissertation verlängert?
5. Er hat schon wieder unser Gespräch unterbrochen.

Exercise 2

1. Die Kinder haben das neue Wort verstanden.
2. Niemand hat Onkel Heinz besucht.
3. Die Soldaten haben das Dorf zerstört.
4. Es ist mir nicht gelungen.
5. Die Katzen sind dem kleinen Mädchen entlaufen.

Exercise 3

Sample answers are given.

1. Er wartet auf einen Freund.
   Wir erwarten einen Brief von unserer Kusine.
2. Martin ist gerade um die Ecke gekommen.
   Ich habe ein Telegramm bekommen.

3. Wir sind zum Park gelaufen.
   Mein Hund ist mir entlaufen.
4. Wer steht an der Ecke?
   Wie ist das Problem entstanden?
5. Wir schreiben einen langen Aufsatz.
   Martin hat seine neue Freundin beschrieben.

Chapter 7

Exercise 1

1. Heute hört der Unterricht um 14 Uhr auf.
   Heute hat der Unterricht um 14 Uhr aufgehört.
2. Das Konzert fängt pünktlich an.
   Das Konzert hat pünktlich angefangen.
3. Warum schlägt das Kind die Tür zu?
   Warum hat das Kind die Tür zugeschlagen?
4. Diese alte Armbanduhr geht oft eine Viertelstunde nach.
   Diese alte Armbanduhr ist oft eine Viertelstunde nachgegangen.
5. Viele Reisende steigen in Frankfurt um.
   Viele Reisende sind in Frankfurt umgestiegen.

Exercise 2

1. Mein Sohn ist täglich um 8 Uhr aufgestanden.
   Mein Sohn wird täglich um 8 Uhr aufstehen.
2. Karin hat ihre neuen Handschuhe angezogen.
   Karin wird ihre neuen Handschuhe anziehen.
3. Die Gäste sind in das Haus eingetreten.
   Die Gäste werden in das Haus eintreten.
4. Viele Passagiere sind am Bahnhof ausgestiegen.
   Viele Passagiere werden am Bahnhof aussteigen.

Exercise 3

Sample answers are given.
1. Wir steigen in den Schlafwagen ein.
2. Sind deine Schwestern mitgekommen?
3. Ich habe den neuen Roman schnell durchgelesen.

4. Machen Sie bitte das Fenster zu!
5. Der Knabe trinkt das Glas Milch aus.

Chapter 8

Exercise 1
1. Bleibt ruhig!
   Bleiben Sie ruhig!
   Ruhig bleiben!
2. Bitte steigt aus!
   Bitte steigen Sie aus!
   Aussteigen bitte!
3. Lacht nicht!
   Lachen Sie nicht!
   Nicht lachen!

Exercise 2
1. Essen wir in einem guten Restaurant!
2. Singen wir Weihnachtslieder!
3. Reparieren wir Omas Wagen!
4. Reisen wir mit dem Bus in die Schweiz!
5. Laufen wir an die Ecke!

Exercise 3
1. Bleiben Sie zurück!
2. Steigen Sie hier aus!
3. Machen Sie das Gepäck auf!
4. Öffnen Sie nicht!

Chapter 9

Exercise 1
1. Ich habe dem Professor eine interessante Frage gestellt.
2. Vor wieviel Jahren ist dein Urgroßvater gestorben?
3. Das junge Pferd ist wieder auf die Wiese gelaufen.

4. Warum bist du so hartnäckig geworden?
5. Gudrun hat die neue Kunsthalle besuchen wollen.

Exercise 2

Sample answers are given.
1. Wir haben unser Haus neulich verkauft.
2. Es ist wirklich sehr kalt geworden.
3. Der Kleine hat die Milch nicht ausgetrunken.
4. Warum bist du da stehengeblieben?
5. Ich habe der netten Frau gedankt.

Exercise 3

1. Ich stand immer um halb sieben auf.
   Ich bin immer um halb sieben aufgestanden.
   Ich werde immer um halb sieben aufstehen.
2. Wer verstand dieses Problem?
   Wer hat dieses Problem verstanden?
   Wer wird dieses Problem verstehen?
3. Wolltest du in die Stadt fahren?
   Hast du in die Stadt fahren wollen?
   Wirst du in die Stadt fahren wollen?

Chapter 10

Exercise 1

1. der Geruch
2. der Glaube(n)
3. der Gesang
4. die Bedeutung
5. die Arbeit
6. das Leben
7. das Gemälde
8. die Wohnung
9. die Abrüstung
10. die Vorsicht

Exercise 2

1. brauchen
2. einkommen
3. erzählen
4. kennen
5. eingehen
6. absehen
7. schauspielen
8. lehren
9. lernen
10. sollen; haben

Exercise 3

1. absehen
2. klingen
3. lehren
4. kämpfen
5. bluten
6. beweisen
7. verdenken *or* verdächtigen
8. ansprechen
9. wechseln
10. merken

Chapter 11

Exercise 1

1. Wir hoffen bestimmt euch bald **zu** besuchen.
2. Wodurch kann man eine fremde Sprache lernen?
3. Es war unmöglich dieses Problem **zu** lösen.
4. Ich habe einen neuen Wagen gekauft, um eine Fahrt nach Paris **zu** machen.
5. Wann wirst du meine Dissertation lesen?
6. Er schweigt, anstatt die Wahrheit **zu** sagen.
7. Sie freuen sich darauf, eine neue Stellung in der Stadt **zu** finden.
8. Es war traurig von einem Verwandten belogen **zu** werden.

9. Die Kinder werden von der Lehrerin gelobt werden.
10. Sie schrie vor Angst, anstatt dem alten Mann **zu** helfen.

Exercise 2

1. Martin warnt seinen Freund sein Geld nicht zu verschwenden.
2. Ich bitte Sie morgen mitzukommen.
3. Das heiße Wetter zwingt uns leichtere Kleidung zu tragen.
4. Frau Bauer forderte von Herrn Braun die Miete zu bezahlen.
5. Ich rate euch langsamer zu essen und zu trinken.
6. Der Chef befiehlt dem neuen Lehrling besser zu arbeiten.
7. Vater erlaubt den Kindern nicht zum Tanz zu gehen.
8. Benno bittet seinen Vater ein Märchen zu lesen.
9. Wir bitten den Professor die Geschichte zu übersetzen.
10. Ich habe ihm geraten einen Rechtsanwalt zu befragen.

Exercise 3

Sample answers are given.

1. Ich komme nach Freiburg, um Jura zu studieren.
2. Es ist nicht möglich den armen Mann zu retten.
3. Er blieb den ganzen Tag im Bett, anstatt Vater zu helfen.
4. Er bittet mich morgen vorbeizukommen.
5. Johann verkaufte das Haus, ohne seine Frau zu fragen.

Chapter 12

Exercise 1

1. Sind deine Eltern in Deutschland geboren?
2. In welchem Jahre wurde Goethe geboren?
3. Luise ist verheiratet. Sie heißt jetzt Luise Dorf, geboren Schuhmann.
4. Bismarck wurde im 19. Jahrhundert geboren.

Exercise 2

1. George Washington wurde (im Jahre) 1732 geboren.
2. Der Tennisspieler Boris Becker ist am 22. November 1967 geboren.

3. Die Zwillinge sind (im Jahre) 2005 geboren.
4. Wolfgang Amadeus Mozart wurde am 27. Januar 1756 geboren.

Chapter 13

Exercise 1
1. zeigend, gezeigt
2. vergehend, vergangen
3. vergessend, vergessen
4. annehmend, angenommen
5. schlafend, geschlafen
6. verbrechend, verbrochen
7. einladend, eingeladen
8. schließend, geschlossen
9. bewegend, bewegt
10. umsteigend, umgestiegen

Exercise 2
1. Die zerbrochene Vase lag auf dem Boden.
2. Sie hat den vorlorenen Ring gefunden.
3. Ein Gesandter wurde nach London geschickt.
4. Die Polizisten holen den ertrunkenen Mann aus dem Wasser heraus.
5. Der Schuhmacher zeigte uns die ausgebesserten Schuhe.
6. Der junge Gelehrte schreibt eine Dissertation.
7. Wohnen deine Verwandten noch in Frankreich?

Chapter 14

Exercise 1
1. versprochen werden
2. getötet werden
3. ausgeschlossen werden
4. angenommen werden
5. gezeigt werden

6. verlernt werden
7. behalten werden
8. komponiert werden

Exercise 2

1. Ein Haus wurde gebaut.
   Ein Haus ist gebaut worden.
   Ein Haus wird gebaut werden.
2. Die Kinder wurden von einem neuen Lehrer unterrichtet.
   Die Kinder sind von einem neuen Lehrer unterrichtet worden.
   Die Kinder werden von einem neuen Lehrer unterrichtet werden.
3. Ihm wurde damit geholfen.
   Ihm ist damit geholfen worden.
   Ihm wird damit geholfen werden.
4. Wurdest du verhaftet?
   Bist du verhaftet worden?
   Wirst du verhaftet werden?

Exercise 3

1. Eine neue Ausstellung wird von dem Studenten besucht.
2. Ein Teller Suppe wurde von der Kellnerin gebracht.
3. Dramen und Gedichte sind von Goethe geschrieben worden.
4. Ihnen ist herzlich gedankt worden.
5. Die neuen Wörter werden von uns gelernt werden.

Chapter 15

Exercise 1

1. er schließe, er schlösse
2. er komme an, er käme an
3. er benehme sich, er benähme sich
4. er kaufe, er kaufte
5. er imponiere, er imponierte
6. er vergesse, er vergässe
7. er beschreibe, er beschriebe

8. er lese durch, er läse durch
9. er zerstöre, er zerstörte
10. er sei, er wäre

Exercise 2

1. Der Mann sagte, dass Karl sich an keinem einzigen Sonntag ausgeruht habe.
2. Der Mann sagte, dass man hier viele Häuser aus Holz baue.
3. Der Mann sagte, dass die Schweizer die Alpen liebten.
4. Der Mann sagte, dass seine Kinder ungeschickt seien.
5. Der Mann sagte, dass der Professor stundenlang über seinen Büchern gesessen habe.

Exercise 3

1. Er tat so, als ob er mich nicht gesehen hätte.
2. Er tat so, als ob seine Frau eine Schönheitskönigin wäre.
3. Er tat so, als ob er sehr reich geworden wäre.
4. Er tat so, als ob er sich mit einer Schauspielerin verheiratet hätte.

Exercise 4

1. Wenn sie nicht gearbeitet hätte, hätte sie kein Geld verdient.
2. Wenn ich Flügel hätte, würde ich wie ein Vogel fliegen.
3. Wenn Vater wieder gesund gewesen wäre, hätte er nach Hause gehen dürfen.
4. Wenn Karl gut Deutsch gesprochen hätte, hätte er die Rede auf deutsch gehalten.
5. Wenn er mehr Zeit hätte, würde er mir oft schreiben.
6. Wenn mein alter Freund mich besuchte, würde ich ihn sofort erkennen.
7. Wenn sie das wüsste, würde sie keine Fragen mehr haben.
8. Wenn ich eine neue Brille hätte, könnte ich alles lesen.

Exercise 5

1. Wir hätten ihn eingeladen, wenn er ein freundlicher Mensch gewesen wäre.
2. Wenn ich das gesagt hätte, hätte ich das gemeint.

3. Wenn er reisen könnte, würde er die Türkei besuchen.
4. Die Arbeiter würden Schach spielen, wenn sie mehr Freizeit hätten.
5. Sie wäre nicht so gemein gewesen, wenn sie mich wirklich geliebt hätte.

Chapter 16

Exercise 1
Sample answers are given.
1. Karin wollte Jura studieren.
2. Die Affen versuchen uns zu imitieren.
3. Seine Ideen haben mir sehr imponiert.
4. Unsere Pläne sind schlecht organisiert.
5. Ich rasiere mich täglich.

Exercise 2
1. spendieren: give a treat
2. photographieren: photograph
3. möblieren: furnish
4. garnieren: garnish
5. hantieren: handle, manipulate
6. isolieren: isolate
7. magnetisieren: magnetize
8. galvanisieren: galvanize
9. mobilisieren: mobilize
10. filtrieren: filter

Exercise 3
1. Die Arbeiter demonstrierten vor dem Rathaus.
   Die Arbeiter haben vor dem Rathaus demonstriert.
   Die Arbeiter werden vor dem Rathaus demonstrieren.
2. Der Knabe verlor seinen Hut.
   Der Knabe hat seinen Hut verloren.
   Der Knabe wird seinen Hut verlieren.